ARCTIC ADVENTURES

Cover photographs by Ian and Sally Wilson
Front Cover: Ian Wilson dogsledding during March on the sea ice of Hudson Bay.
Back Cover: Ian and Sally Wilson canoeing the Thelon Canyon . . . taken with a remote control.

Our sincere thanks to:

B.C.T.V.
Molson Breweries
Altamira Investment Services
Canadian Northern Shield Insurance

for their generous support
of our Arctic Adventures

ARCTIC ADVENTURES

Exploring Canada's North by Canoe and Dog Team

Text and Photographs by

Ian & Sally Wilson

Illustrations by Sally Tatlow Wilson

Gordon Soules Book Publishers Ltd.

West Vancouver, Canada

Seattle, USA

**With special thanks to Maureen Colclough
for all her help with this book**

Text © 1992 by Ian Wilson
Illustrations © 1992 by Sally Tatlow Wilson

This book is printed on acid-free paper.

Published in Canada by
Gordon Soules Book Publishers Ltd.
1352-B Marine Drive
West Vancouver, B.C.
Canada V7T 1B5

Published in the U.S.A. by
Gordon Soules Book Publishers Ltd.
620 - 1916 Pike Place
Seattle, WA 98101

Canadian Cataloguing in Publishing Data

Wilson, Ian, 1955–
Arctic adventures

Includes index
ISBN 0-919574-43-2

1. Northwest Territories—Description and travel—1981–
2. Canoes and canoeing—Northwest Territories
3. Dogsledding—Northwest Territories
4. Inuit—Northwest Territories—Social life and customs.
I. Wilson, Sally, 1955–   II. Title
FC4167.3.W54 1992   917.19'2043   C92-091489-6
F1060.W54 1992

Edited by Anne Norman
Cover design by Harry Bardal
Printed and bound in Canada by Gagne Book Manufacturers

C O N T E N T S

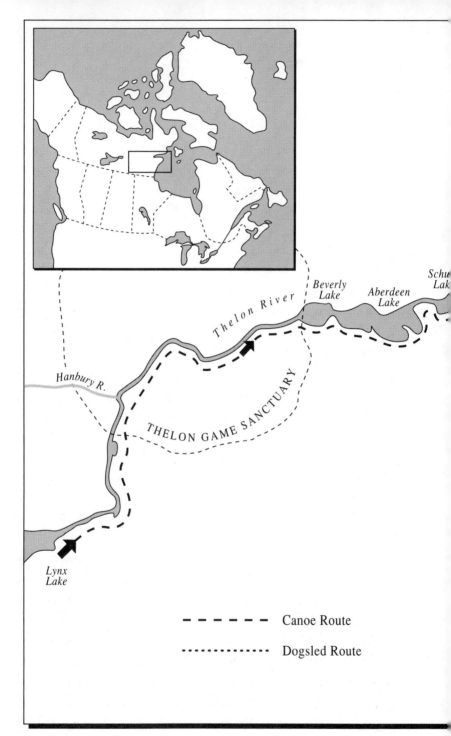

Schu
Lak

Beverly
Lake

Aberdeen
Lake

Thelon River

Hanbury R.

THELON GAME SANCTUARY

Lynx
Lake

- - - - - Canoe Route

··········· Dogsled Route

Route of Expedition

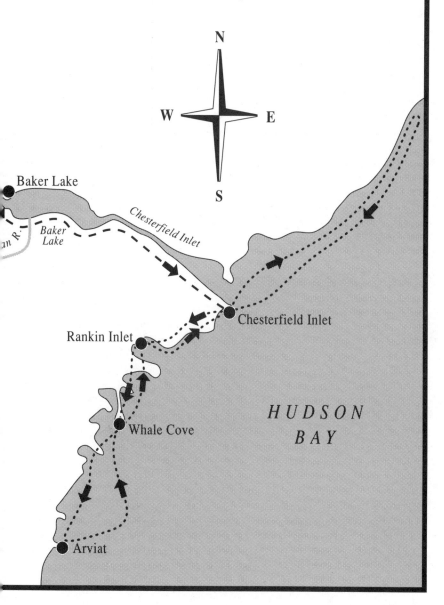

Prologue

The musty smell of canvas filled my nostrils as Sally and I rummaged through a pile of tents. Nearby, the grizzled denim-clad owner of the camping supply store leaned against a rack of snowshoes.

"Let's see if I've got this straight," the old-timer said as he surveyed the pile of supplies we had selected. "You're planning to go on a year-long trek across the Arctic by canoe and dog team."

"That about sums it up," I said, steeling myself for the questions I knew would follow. The old-timer had always taken an interest in our adventures and misadventures.

"And you tell me your whitewater canoeing is a little shaky, your wife is scared of dogs, and you've never even had a pet mutt before," he continued, looking me straight in the eye.

I reminded him that we had managed to tackle several demanding rivers on previous trips. Sally added that she was sure she would get over her fear of dogs once she got to know them. Then, almost as an afterthought, I assured him that we would learn what we needed to know along the way.

I hoped that I looked as confident as my words sounded.

"How about the winter—setting up camp in a blizzard at minus forty? You must like winter camping a whole lot," he replied. His banter would have seemed more caustic if I hadn't noticed him wink at Sally.

Undeterred by his good-natured scepticism, I rattled on about our plans to charter a bush plane from Yellowknife in the Northwest Territories to the headwaters of the Thelon River. From there we would canoe for almost three months until we reached Hudson Bay. Our canoe route would take us through twelve hundred kilometres of the Barren Lands, passing only one isolated community along the way.

When we reached Hudson Bay, we planned to learn the skills necessary to survive the harsh northern winter. Then we hoped to acquire a team of Huskies and travel by dog team for almost two thousand kilometres. For us, it was the ultimate challenge. It was the spark of an idea that had been fanned into action after years of campfire talks.

"Well, where are your maps?" the old-timer asked finally. "You always show me your maps."

Sally and I eagerly unrolled our maps across the floor. Piece by piece, the old-timer dismantled his store display, placing a boot on one corner of a map, a shiny camp pot on another. By the time he had finished, half his display was on the floor, holding down our collection of maps, which lay end to end across the room.

"Hmmm. One inch equals four miles—not much detail here. A fifty-foot drop in the river doesn't even show," he said. Unfortunately, that was the only scale map available for the remote area we were going to.

His finger traced the blue line of the Thelon River across ten maps. The river sprawled across an endless expanse of the Barrens, well north of the dotted line that stated "Approximate Northern Limit of Trees." The Thelon began among a network of lakes deep in the Precambrian Shield northeast of Great Slave Lake. By the second map, the river had telltale black lines across it, indicating impassable rapids. Farther north it passed through four massive lakes and finally widened to a long inlet on its way to Hudson Bay.

"Looks easy on the maps. They only take up half my shop," he commented as we surveyed the sheets.

He looked closely at the fine print and asked us how confident we were canoeing an ever-changing river guided only by maps drawn more than thirty-five years ago. Then with a wicked grin, he read out the disclaimer on the map stating that magnetic compasses were inaccurate in this area.

Moments later, the front door opened. "Darn! A customer. They always come when I'm busy."

On seeing the maps on the floor, the customer seemed to forget what he had come for. He knelt down, asking what our plans were.

The old-timer answered for us. "Well, they're going to start here in grizzly country, wander for three months through nothing but swamps and mosquitoes, and end up in polar bear territory for the winter."

I added a few details for the benefit of the visitor, who simply shook his head.

"How many people are going? Who's guiding you?"

"Just Sally and me. We'll find our own way."

Our plans were not quite as farfetched as they sounded. Several years ago, Sally and I had built a log cabin deep in the wilderness of northern British Columbia and lived there for fourteen months. Since then, we had been on many extended wilderness trips. Although Sally and I had never been to the Arctic before, we had spent months planning and packing for this trip.

We tried to explain why we were going: to photograph northern wildlife, to learn about the Inuit ways, and to experience the Arctic through four seasons. Perhaps this list was just a way to define our motives for other people. The real reason for going could be boiled down to three words: for the adventure.

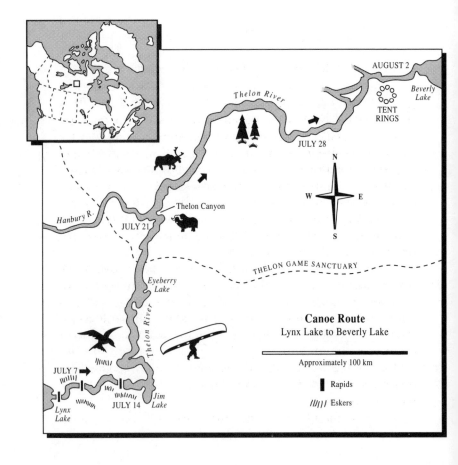

AUGUST 2

Thelon River

Beverly Lake

TENT RINGS

JULY 28

Hanbury R.

JULY 21

Thelon Canyon

N
W   E
S

THELON GAME SANCTUARY

Eyeberry Lake

Thelon River

Canoe Route
Lynx Lake to Beverly Lake

Approximately 100 km

JULY 7

▮ Rapids

///||/ Eskers

JULY 14

Jim Lake

Lynx Lake

ONE

Canoeing North

Through the green haze of our mosquito head nets, Sally and I surveyed our surroundings. The tundra flowed as far as we could see in every direction: a thin moss-and-lichen blanket spread over a bed of permafrost. Sweeps of white sandy eskers and countless small blue ponds gave the scene a patchwork-quilt appearance.

It was July 7, and we had just been dropped off by a float plane near the headwaters of the Thelon River. Our gear lay in a jumbled pile on the beach.

"You won't find any place wilder than this," Sally said, taking a deep breath of the cool, clear air. From where we stood on the beach, there was no end to the wilderness. The land looked vast and empty, and the sky seemed to go on forever, larger and somehow more humbling than a skyline of towering mountains.

"I see why this is called the Barrens," I said, as much to myself as to Sally. She was too busy searching through our packs to respond.

"Do you know where the bug juice is?" Sally asked, swatting at her neck and shoulders.

A hundred pinpricks of mosquitoes stabbing through my shirt prompted me to join Sally in the search. I dived towards the pile of gear to find the repellent and our bug jackets. The winged welcoming committee had arrived!

"We're probably the only humans in five hundred kilometres, and those mosquitoes are hungry!" Sally said.

"Once we start canoeing we'll leave them behind," I replied, eager to begin our journey down the river.

Before we could paddle away from the hordes, we had to squeeze a mountain of gear into our small canoe. Sally and I had never travelled with such a load before—sixty days' worth of food and supplies. Enough, we hoped, to keep us going until we reached our resupply point at Baker Lake, more than eight hundred kilometres by paddle and portage. We had tested the load by packing most of it into the canoe before leaving Vancouver, but extra items added at the last minute made the pile look enormous.

The three food bags were so heavy that I could barely lift even one. I wrestled them into the middle of the boat, and then placed a backpack just behind Sally's seat in the bow. At my feet went a waterproof clothes bag and another pack. Sally crammed two fuel cans and rainwear into the space behind my seat; the area underneath each seat was already filled by waterproof boxes of camera gear.

We spent nearly an hour arranging the packs and bags in different positions. Finally we jammed the fishing rod, tent poles, and other odd-shaped items into the last gaps we could find.

"Will there be any room left for me?" Sally teased when she caught me stuffing a boot on each side of her seat.

"Sure, no problem," I said. I decided to wait until she was preoccupied with tying in the packs before placing our bulky tripod where her feet would go.

We managed to squeeze everything in, but the canoe was loaded to the bursting point. I laced a rope back and forth across the canoe to secure the gear and compress the load. It was still a struggle to stretch the nylon spray deck over the bulging packs.

After we settled into our seats, Sally pushed our over-loaded craft from shore. I picked up my shiny new paddle from the spray deck.

"Ready?" I asked. In unison, we dug our paddles into the water.

"That's one," Sally said. "Only six zillion strokes to go until we reach Hudson Bay!"

After months of planning, it felt great to be on the river. From the stern of the canoe, I looked past Sally and down the river to the horizon, wondering what adventures lay ahead in the coming year. I remembered reading about an explorer who said that people shouldn't have adventures, only experiences. Funny, I thought, it was adventure we were looking forward to.

Within two hours Sally and I were bobbing unsteadily down the first set of small rapids. The loaded canoe was unresponsive in the fast water, so different from the way our sleek fibreglass and Kevlar craft usually performed. A wave washed over the deck; I reached out with my paddle and held it flat on the surface of the river to stabilize the canoe.

"One problem with loading the canoe like a freight barge," I said as the river flushed us into calmer water, "is that it steers like one!"

I calculated that the total weight of passengers and cargo aboard our overloaded craft was more than three hundred kilograms. No wonder the canoe felt a little sluggish! It would take some time to hone our paddling skills and get used to the loaded canoe.

"We'll have to begin our turns sooner and lean with the canoe more," Sally said at the end of the day.

"That should work . . . as long as we don't lean *too* much!" I replied.

That evening Sally and I wandered across the tundra and became two small specks on the vast land. We enjoyed the solitude and silence, but we still felt overwhelmed by the endless open space.

"It feels lonely out here," I said, taking Sally's hand in mine.

At each rest stop through the day, I had scanned the horizon for something to focus on, something to break up the limitless landscape. The land looked so empty. We had come to the north prepared for the physical challenges of this trip, but we hadn't expected the vastness of the Barrens to feel so intimidating.

I happened to glance down, and there, almost under my boot, was a small cluster of delicate pink flowers. Looking more carefully, we found a rich tapestry of colours and shapes close to the ground. In sheltered hollows were white clusters of flowering Labrador tea, mats of pink moss campion, and bunches of bright yellow cinquefoil, all only a few centimetres high.

The spell of intimidation was broken; the tundra was certainly vast, but it was not empty. I relaxed and took a deep breath. The air was fragrant with a faint, delicate aroma of flowers, dried caribou moss crushed by our boots, and sun-warmed crowberry plants.

Sally and I sat down among the flowers and felt the tension of the past months slowly drain away. The weeks before our departure had been a mad panic to research our route, sort equipment, and make final arrangements. As our July departure date drew closer, we had worked almost round the clock, purchasing and packing food for the year, sewing bags for camping supplies, and making last-minute adjustments to equipment. Now the only frantic buzz of activity was from the cloud of mosquitoes that hovered around us. The only other sound was the light scratch of Sally's pencil on paper as she sketched the tranquil scene.

Although it was ten o'clock by the time we had our tent set up, the sun was still high above the horizon. It felt odd to go to bed with bright sunlight streaming into the tent. To bask in this abundance of daylight was like discovering a new world, where the normal rhythms of life were suspended. We lay wide awake, gazing through the screened tent door until the sun dipped towards the horizon at eleven o'clock.

"Is that rain I hear?" Sally asked sleepily at six the next morning.

"Can't be," I said. "It's a sauna in here!" Through the thin nylon walls, I could see the bright sun, already high above the horizon. And yet we could hear what sounded like rain pelting against the nylon walls.

As our senses slowly wakened, it dawned on us that the "raindrops" were hundreds of mosquitoes and black flies battering the tent. We pulled on head nets and slapped on insect repellent before heading out to brave the needle-nosed creatures that waited eagerly for blood.

After a breakfast of mosquitoes in oatmeal, we walked around the next bend in the river to see what was in store for us. We had hoped for an easy start to the day but found a boulder-strewn stretch of water.

"What do you think? Maybe we should portage," Sally said, eyeing the boulders.

"Sounds good to me. I'm not keen about playing boulder-billiards with a loaded canoe," I replied.

We both knew that adventure involved risks, but they had to be calculated ones; everything we depended on to survive in the Barrens rode with us in the canoe. The river was still shallow with exposed boulders, and we couldn't afford to swamp the canoe and lose our gear. We would have many opportunities to paddle non-stop farther downriver when tributaries added depth and volume to the Thelon.

By the third of five trips across the portage, we began to feel like cross-country furniture movers. I plodded along in a daze, my head deep in the belly of the upturned canoe. Clouds of black flies accompanied me under the canoe, where they were sheltered from the wind. Even though I wore my head net and bug jacket, flies found their way through small openings at my neck and sleeves. I could feel them tickling my skin as they crawled around looking for the juiciest part to bite. Each bite drew blood, dotting my shirt with red. My hands were occupied holding the canoe, and there was nothing I could do about my tormentors.

"How are the mosquitoes out there?" I asked as Sally trudged past me with her load, her jacket fluttering in the wind.

"You have them all!" she said, sounding quite pleased about the situation.

"Wait till your turn under this mosquito trap!"

On the next trip across, I struggled with a thirty-five kilogram pack. At least it was easier to carry than the canoe, and my view had expanded immensely—from the inside of a canoe hull to the entire tundra.

Because I carried the heavy food bags, Sally burdened herself with the awkward things. After loading her pack with as many loose odds and ends as possible, Sally heaved it onto her back and stumbled off at a fast walk. Runners, binoculars, and pots tied to the outside of her pack swung freely from side to side. Tent poles, a tripod, and a red life jacket bulged out of the overstuffed pack towering over her head. Her arms were laden with paddles and another life jacket.

"You look like a beginner backpacker gone berserk," I said, chuckling at the sight of Sally's bulging load.

"And *you* look like the hunchback of Notre Dame," Sally replied, as I walked, bent over, beside her.

Over the next four days, we had to portage the canoe six times past rock-strewn rapids. On one particularly difficult portage, Sally and I trudged along in silence, both hot, tired, and bothered by swarming mosquitoes. I became even more dispirited when I remembered the maps, which indicated that most of our portages would occur early in the trip when our packs were the heaviest.

Once we were back on the river, our outlook improved. We enjoyed the thrill of paddling fast water and running a small set of rapids.

"I've forgotten the portage already," Sally said. "I guess two requirements for northern adventure are a strong back and a weak memory."

We decided that portages were just part of the Barren Lands experience. As long as we paddled more than we portaged, Sally and I couldn't complain. This was, after all, a wilderness river and we didn't expect the trip to be easy.

As the Thelon wound through the tundra, its character

Surveying the route ahead

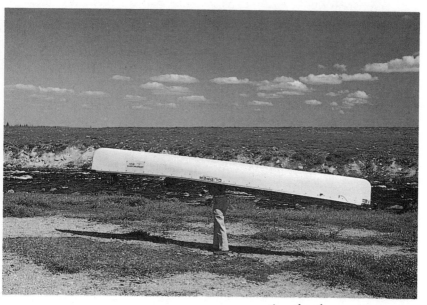

Another long portage

alternated between narrow, turbulent passages and wide, lazy stretches. Our days began to take on the rhythm of the river. Each time the river gained speed, our paddling tempo reflected the energy of the fast water. On the slower stretches of smooth water, we could lay our paddles down, lean back, and gaze across the vast landscape.

With each day, we felt the pace of the river increase as more tributaries added volume to the Thelon. By our eighth day on the river, we were 160 kilometres from the headwaters. The Thelon had grown to a vibrant waterway.

Late that afternoon, Sally stopped paddling in mid-stroke and turned her head, listening intently.

"Do you hear that?" she asked.

I stopped paddling and listened. There was no mistaking the dull roar of churning water. Nervously I unfolded the map. It showed no impassable rapids, no telltale narrowing of the river—yet we could hear the sound of whitewater. Sally leaned out and thrust her paddle into the water, pulling the bow left towards the shore.

Sally and I walked along the shoreline and studied the river, reading the rapids as we searched for passages that were clear of boulders. In particular, we were looking for obstacles that we might not notice from canoe-level, such as the V-shaped swirls of water that indicated barely submerged boulders.

The roar that had alerted us came from one set of exposed rocks, which could be bypassed with some careful canoeing. This was the first lengthy stretch of rapids we had come to, and I looked over to Sally to gauge her reaction. She took a long look at the river and then turned to me.

"Looks like some exciting paddling for tomorrow. It should be a blast!" she said, smiling broadly.

Whitewater

Sally and I buckled our life jackets and tightened the spray skirts around our waists in preparation for the long stretch of whitewater. Then we reviewed our route.

"Okay," Sally said, looking down the river. "We start down the left, beside the big boulder. Then ferry across and take the smooth water mid-river until the next rapids."

We talked it out, surveying the rapids from the canoe and comparing the view to what we had seen during our walk along the shoreline.

"What about the rock below the chute?" I asked.

"What rock? Oh, *that* one!"

We discussed the route in more detail and finally agreed on a plan. Once we were paddling, there would no time for a mid-rapid conference.

After the drudgery of seven long portages, I was ready for some excitement. In my mind I canoed the river, practising the strokes required. I wrapped my fingers tightly around the paddle and took a deep breath.

"Let's go for it!" I called.

Sally thrust her paddle into the river and pulled the canoe

into the fast water. As soon as the current caught the canoe, my heartbeat quickened. I could feel the adrenalin pumping through my body as we manoeuvred the canoe towards the rapids. Backpaddling so that we wouldn't pick up too much speed, we slid along, bumping lightly against a boulder. Then came a turn to the right, followed by a knee-high drop of foaming water.

"Rock! Draw left!" Our voices communicated the level of urgency for each move as we worked our way down the rapids.

Although we yelled encouragement back and forth in the wildest sections, I usually followed Sally's strokes without exchanging words. Her job was to watch for rocks and then pull or pry with her paddle to avoid them. My job was to make sure the stern of the canoe followed her route and remained pointing straight down the river. We worked as a team—if Sally pried with her paddle, I pulled mine towards me to move the canoe across the river.

I could see Sally's shoulders tense as she concentrated fully on the river. Together, we powered through or back-paddled in the fast water, as the situation dictated. We used the strong current of the river to our advantage: to steer our craft, to maintain control.

We sped down the river, paddles flashing in the sun and a refreshing spray from the waves cooling our flushed faces. At the bottom of the rapids, Sally looked over her shoulder. I flashed her a wide grin. This was adventure in its raw form: pure, unrefined, heart-thumping thrills. The river slowed again and our heartbeats returned to normal.

Fifteen minutes downriver we pulled out again to survey another set of rapids. Sally and I spent some time examining the boiling whitewater. It was beyond paddling. We groaned in unison at the thought of another portage.

"Let's line the canoe," Sally suggested. "It beats carrying everything."

We walked along the shore, carefully controlling the bow and stern lines to work our canoe around each obstacle. In other places, we waded through the frigid water, gripping the side of the canoe. As we wrestled the canoe down the rapids, we felt the power of the river pushing against our legs. Finally we climbed back into the canoe to enjoy a kilometre of white, rolling water, free of obstacles.

"Yee-haw!" I yelled as the canoe blasted through a set of rollers. Sally's enthusiasm seemed a bit dampened—a huge wave had completely drenched her as she leaned out to draw the canoe sideways. I heard her shout something about needing a snorkel as another wave washed over the bow.

"I think the canoe is a bit bow-heavy," I said when we shot from the waves into still water. After we pulled ashore, I slid the heavy food bags farther back in the canoe to redistribute the weight. Meanwhile Sally changed into dry clothes.

For three more action-packed days, we canoed down fast, foaming whitewater. Then the Thelon River spilled into a small lake. The change was startling; one minute we were plunging through wet and wild rapids, the next we were floating across calm water. The lake reminded us of some tropical paradise, with white sandy beaches, sand dunes, and sparkling blue water. The illusion ended when we looked beyond the lake to the barren tundra of grass and rock. As we canoed to the beach, we noticed wolf prints and caribou tracks along the sandy shoreline.

It was the third week of July and birds had claimed the wetlands for the short summer nesting season. The lake was busy with winged visitors, ranging from terns and jaegers to ducks and loons. From the low growth along the shoreline, sparrows and thrushes proclaimed their territories. As we walked along the sandy beach, plovers and sandpipers scooted out of our way.

The warmth of the afternoon sun encouraged us to take a fast but necessary dip in the lake. The water was warm, at least the top few centimetres were. Below that it was numbing. I let out an impressive Tarzan yodel as the frigid water hit my body. We soaped, scrubbed, and rinsed in record time.

The moment we emerged from the water a horde of blood-thirsty mosquitoes descended upon us. We dressed quickly, while performing a towel-swinging, running, jumping bug-dance. I looked over to Sally, and wondered if I looked as hilarious as she did, with one foot in her pants as she slapped at mosquitoes and hopped about like a hyperactive aerobics instructor.

"Sponge baths in the tent were never that action-packed!" Sally said as she scratched the new bites on her arm.

Soon after the lake, the river regained momentum. Ahead we could see that the Thelon was dropping fast and there was some turbulent whitewater.

"River left looks clear," Sally called over her shoulder.

I worked hard to keep the canoe pointing straight down river, countering the cross-waves and chop that tried to push us in all directions. In the bow, Sally had an exciting ride as the canoe rode up on the crest of standing waves, then crashed down. Each time a wave washed over the front of the canoe, I heard Sally shout with joy. At least I think it was joy; the noise of the surging rapids was too loud for me to hear what she was saying. One particularly high wave tore the spray skirt off her suspenders and dumped what must have felt like half the river into her lap.

"Ai-yai! Those waves were HUGE!" she said, emptying her spray skirt at the end of the run.

"Is your Tilley hat wet?"

"No."

"Then they weren't *that* big!" I replied.

That evening we stopped early as the sky darkened and raindrops spattered the river. At three in the morning, the noise of flapping nylon added some variety to the rhythmic drumming of rain. I got up and raced around in my shorts, placing boulders on the tent pegs to hold the tent down in the gusting wind.

When Sally woke at a more reasonable hour, the rain had stopped and the wind had dwindled to intermittent gusts. After peering out the tent door, she nudged me awake.

We had just finished loading the canoe when it started to rain again. An hour later, heavy rain began drumming noisily on the taut spray deck of the canoe. To keep warm,

Sally and I paddled hard all day. We ate soggy snacks in the rain, paddled in the rain, stretched our legs in the rain.

That evening as I dug through the waterproof food bag in search of supper, I appreciated the time and effort we had spent packaging each meal before we started our trip.

"How about chicken curry?" I called out.

"Sounds great. What colour Kool-Aid goes with chicken?" Sally called from the river, where she was getting water.

All the dried ingredients for our supper were in one small plastic bag: freeze-dried chicken, rice, sliced almonds, peas, onions, and curry powder. Every meal for the entire year was prepared in this way, from pancake breakfasts to three-course suppers.

It may not have been gourmet fare, but it was fast. Just ten minutes after I poured the mixture into a pot, we were huddled together under a small tarp, eating our supper. A moment later, the wind rustled the tarp and a stream of cold water poured into our pot of chicken curry. This meal tested our resolve never to eat in our tent for fear of four-legged visitors.

"What a choice—to eat supper crouched under a piece of plastic or be visited by a bear in the night," Sally said after supper. She pushed her empty bowl out into the pouring rain to be rinsed.

Once in the tent, Sally and I reviewed our day's progress. We stretched a length of string along the map, following our route. Then I measured it against the scale on the bottom of the map. One grid was equal to ten kilometres, and a two-grid day was our goal. Our itinerary was based on a twenty-kilometre-a-day average to allow for delays due to wind, weather, and portages. This schedule also gave us time to photograph the scenery and any animals that we saw along the way.

"A three-grid day!" I reported after measuring the string. We had been on the river for two weeks, but the portages had made it difficult to meet our daily goal of twenty kilometres. We were pleased with our progress during the past few days on the faster water.

The next morning, the sky had cleared. As we continued down the river, I thought of how peaceful the Barrens seemed when the sun was out, compared to how cold and unwelcoming it had felt the day before.

Above us, terns played on the wind currents, much like we played in the current of the river. On outstretched wings they drifted, held their position, or turned gracefully. Their flight seemed effortless, like feathers floating in the air.

We canoed past a tern colony on a small island just downriver. Several terns aggressively defended the nesting area, diving and hitting our hats with their bills when we paddled too close. But their most effective defence was to bomb us with droppings.

"A direct hit!" I laughed loudly when an aerial projectile splattered on Sally's hat. I laughed too soon. On the next pass, a tern sprayed me with foul, fishy-smelling excrement, which dripped down the front of my mosquito head net. I yanked off the head net and stuffed it under the spray deck, where it remained until we stopped to check out a lengthy set of rapids.

We had reached the Thelon Canyon, almost three hundred kilometres from where we had started paddling. Getting past the canyon required a long portage. We pulled ashore in a backwater bordered by thick willows.

Before we began the portage, Sally and I climbed a high hill to view the river. Below us, whitewater surged in deep rocky gorges and chutes that sent waves boiling high up the walls of the canyon. Chasms of white, foaming water extended for as far as we could see. My eye followed the rim of the canyon until I saw a peregrine falcon soar over the top, hover, and then dive, its wings folded back like a grey-feathered arrow.

As we carried the first load of gear along the portage, we marvelled at the spectacular view. The canyon walls were of red and yellow sandstone, contrasting sharply with the white water below and azure-blue sky above. Strange water-carved gargoyles and tall pillars adorned the east bank.

By the following afternoon, we had carried our five loads

across the tundra. The distance between where we took the canoe out and put it back into the river was only two kilometres. But after traipsing back and forth with all our loads, we ended up walking almost twenty kilometres across the portage.

"That was exhausting. I think we deserve a double ration of fruit cake," I gasped, flopping down onto the moss.

"And a Mars Bar!" Sally added. I began salivating like Pavlov's dog and my eyes bulged in disbelief when Sally produced a disfigured, half-melted bar that she had hoarded in her pack for two weeks. It was amazing how a mere chocolate bar could boost our morale.

We had portaged only partway through the canyon. A tangle of willows and a barrier of car-sized boulders made it impossible to portage around the last stretch of rapids.

The next morning, we studied the river.

"We could stay on this side and shoot the rapids," Sally suggested. "Or we could canoe across to the far side and paddle our way down between the shelves and boulders."

Neither option sounded appealing.

"What if we don't make it across?" I wondered aloud. The water looked menacing, foaming over and around countless boulders. Even if we avoided those boulders, there were still enormous waves to deal with.

We walked along the right bank to scout the rapids and discovered a narrow ledge beside the surging water.

"How about walking along this ledge and working the canoe down with ropes?" I asked, hoping that the ledge wouldn't be too slippery to walk along while holding the canoe.

It seemed to be our best option. To keep our clothes dry, we stripped down to underwear, life jackets, and runners.

With ten-metre-long tracking ropes tied to each end of the canoe, we each held a line in our right hand and gripped the side of the canoe in the other. Then we walked, waded, and scrambled along the shore. Once we reached the ledge, we jumped from rock to rock until the canoe was at the brink of the most turbulent water.

"No problem!" Sally called back to me as the loaded canoe floated down the shallow water beside us.

We were only halfway along the ledge when Sally stepped to the right around a bend and pulled the canoe with her. This caused my end of the canoe to swing out into the river, exposing it to the chute. The fast water caught the canoe, nearly wrenching me off my feet. I tried to hold the canoe, but it was almost sideways to the current and about to be pulled under.

"Hey!" I shouted. Sally turned around and saw my predicament.

"I've got it," she yelled over the roar. I was being pulled farther and farther out into the current. Should I let go or swim with the canoe?

"Let go!" Sally called. I released the rope and watched helplessly as the canoe swung broadside to the current. The canoe would have swamped if I'd held on for even one more second. I hoped that Sally really did have the canoe—without it, we would be stranded, hundreds of kilometres from anywhere.

Sally was braced on a dry rock and held the line tightly with both hands. Somehow she managed to hold on as the canoe swung around in the current and dropped down the waist-high falls.

The canoe was still upright! Our canoe with its precious cargo was drawn into an eddy and settled on the quiet water.

"Great job, partner," I said, hugging her so tightly I would have bruised her ribs if she hadn't been wearing a bulky life jacket. "But I think our technique needs a little work."

THREE

Life on the Tundra

"Lunch?" Sally asked as she rummaged around in the grub bag behind her seat. While I continued to paddle, she prepared a snack from our floating deli. Then her paddle inched towards me—a serving platter laden with bannock, salami, and cheese.

We drifted down the river, the late-July sun warming our backs. It was hard to imagine that only the day before we had been lining our canoe around the falls in the shadow of the Thelon Canyon. Now we were basking in the sunlight of a broad valley and the smooth, green water was broken by just a few riffles.

"What's that on the shore?" I asked a few minutes later, pointing my piece of bannock to a cluster of oddly placed black spots.

"Just rocks," Sally replied, barely glancing up.

As the current carried us closer, the "rocks" began to move. Muskoxen! Several bulky, black mounds of fur ambled slowly along the shoreline. Dining on willow leaves and grasses, the muskoxen kept their heads down. There was no telling which end was which.

Sally and I beached the canoe so that we could photograph the closest animal, which was resting behind a clump of willows. We walked in a bent-over position, moving from willow to willow for camouflage. When we finally stood up, we were only twenty paces away. The muskox still wasn't aware of us.

"I don't think we should startle him," I whispered. "I'm sure those sharp horns aren't just for decoration." We talked in louder and louder voices hoping to make our presence known.

Cautiously, I took a few more steps towards the muskox. The animal was snoring, and a great stentorian rumbling filled the air.

"How close do you want to get?" Sally called from behind me.

At the sound of her voice, the muskox woke and lurched to its feet. I froze in my tracks when the bull marched straight towards me. I became even more concerned when the other animals instinctively followed the old bull.

In my mind I quickly reviewed everything I had read about these creatures. It didn't amount to much, but I did remember that if they felt threatened they would either form a defensive circle . . . or attack. I hoped it would be the former.

The bull thrashed a bush with his horns and rubbed a foreleg on his nose while uttering threatening grunts. Now I remembered—this was the precursor to a charge. The bull lowered his head and advanced with a very deliberate, stiff-legged walk.

Fortunately the muskox was bluffing. A few steps later, the bull stopped to feed, stripping leaves off a willow branch. From relative safety behind a boulder, we watched the herd of animals. My gaze was fixed on the two large horns of the old bull. They grew out of a solid plate of bone on his forehead, circling forward to sharp, shiny points. The bull was no taller than a pony, but thick hair flowing down to his knees, high shoulders, and intimidating horns made him appear massive.

As I moved the tripod closer for a better photograph, the metal clunked against a boulder. This unusual noise galvanized the animals to action and the herd loped across the tundra. Like locomotives with fur coats, the muskoxen thundered away, the ground shaking under their hoofs.

Watching the muskoxen had been like stepping thousands of years back in time. Their appearance reminded me of drawings I had seen of the great woolly mammoths—the giants that had died out eons ago. The presence of the prehistoric-looking muskoxen reinforced the feeling of being in a land that time, and humans, had not yet altered.

Over the next week, Sally and I saw several small groups of muskoxen as we continued down the river. They seemed to congregate in the lush, green growth along this stretch of the Thelon River. We were passing through the Thelon Game Sanctuary, a huge wilderness area set aside as a preserve for muskoxen. Pockets of spruce, fields of knee-high cotton grass, and clusters of waist-high fireweed plants grew along the river bank. After we had paddled more than three hundred kilometres past tundra of glaciated rock and ground-hugging growth, it was a visual treat to see this oasis of green.

We drifted past a grove of trees, savouring the smell of sun-warmed spruce needles and marvelling at this growth, hundreds of kilometres north of the tree line. Suddenly a grizzly bear burst from the willows along the shoreline. We stopped paddling and sat motionless, each holding our breath.

The bronze-coloured giant saw us, and for an instant it probably wondered what the strange yellow object floating on the river was. Then, without warning, the grizzly charged down the embankment straight towards us. We were only a few metres from the shore. That was uncomfortably close to a bear who took its strides at two metres each.

Sally and I exchanged nervous glances. There was no need for words. Together, we dug our paddles into the river, thrashing furiously in the water as we struggled to widen the distance between us and the advancing bear.

The sight of our flashing paddles must have startled the bear. When I glanced over my shoulder to check our progress, the grizzly had halted and was studying us from the shore. The huge animal was standing on its rear legs and sniffing the air in loud snorts. Then the bear spun around and bolted up the hill.

"Perhaps we need a bath. That bear took off pretty fast when it smelled us," Sally said with a grin.

The encounter with the grizzly was fresh in our minds when we stopped for the night. Sally and I took great care to look for signs of bear along the beach, and we set up camp only when we were both satisfied that the area was bear-free.

At four in the morning, a grunting noise startled us from our sleep. Our first thought was that the grizzly had found us and was helping itself to our food. We lay motionless for many long minutes hoping the sound would go away. It didn't.

Slowly, quietly, we unzipped the tent door and then peered out into the dull light of an overcast morning. The grunting continued.

"Can you see anything?" I whispered.

"No bears, but I can't figure out what the noise is."

A moment later Sally jabbed my side.

"What?" I whispered hoarsely.

"Caribou. Maybe forty of them among the rocks on the opposite shore."

We dressed quickly, grabbing the cameras and binoculars on our way out of the tent. As our eyes adjusted to the low light, we noticed more and more animals. I was transfixed; the land itself seemed to be moving. The greyish brown mounds that we had thought were boulders started to move. Then the "bushes" also began moving. We revised our estimate to several hundred animals as more and more came over the hilltop.

"Look at them all. This is fantastic!" I said.

We could hardly believe our luck. Photographing the barren-ground caribou migration was high on our "wish list." But during the three weeks we had been travelling across the Barrens, we had seen only a straggler or two.

Sally and I canoed across the river and landed below the main cluster of caribou. All we saw was a wall of dark shapes moving slowly across the meadow. A tangle of black antlers rising above the horizon was silhouetted against the sky like branches of trees.

The caribou did not seem concerned as we walked closer. Some snorted and moved away, but their places were quickly filled by other curious animals as they formed a loose circle around us. Several caribou were only a few paces from us.

The silence of the calm morning was broken by the low grunting of cows and calves calling to each other. Hundreds of eyes stared at us with intense curiosity. Some cows sniffed and tentatively approached us. Calves and yearlings ventured closer, their nostrils flaring as they pushed through the herd of animals. They peered at us and sniffed the air. The bravest took a few more steps in our direction and sniffed again, but even those usually jumped and turned in one motion in their hurry to return to the safety of the herd.

We began to feel a new energy in the group. The animals down by the river had started to move. Like brown floodwater, the caribou poured down the hill to the river; the entire hill was a moving mass of brown.

Without hesitating, each animal plunged into the water and started to swim across, some in groups, others alone. Sally and I rushed to the canoe and paddled back across the river.

The river was thick with animals. Calves nosed up against the downstream flank of their mothers; each calf swam in the protected wake of its mother. The muscular bulls didn't have the same buoyancy as the females. They sank up to their shoulders, and we could see only their necks, heads, and towering antlers moving across the river.

As soon as their hoofs touched ground again, the caribou started trotting, splashing water high in the air and

A prehistoric-looking muskox

Caribou crossing the Thelon River

creating a deafening roar like a waterfall. The noise reached a crescendo when the caribou broke into a run near the shore. The sound changed to dull thudding as the herd ran up the sandy beach, not far from our camp.

Silver droplets of water were highlighted by the morning sun as many animals stopped briefly to shake water from their fur. Then they began a graceful trot that seemed so effortless and smooth.

As the column of caribou approached the shore where we were standing, it fanned out and then engulfed and flowed around us. I took my eye from the camera viewfinder and gazed at the constant flow of animals. I felt dwarfed by the immense spectacle before us, overwhelmed by the sights, sounds, and smells of the migration. In every direction, we saw a mass of moving animals. The noise of the thundering hoofs was blended with continuous grunts, mostly from cows calling to their calves. The air was heavy with the musty smell of damp fur. These caribou were the lifeblood of the Barrens.

By mid-afternoon the bulk of the herd had passed. We estimated that there had been a steady procession of roughly forty caribou a minute crossing the river for more than six hours. That added up to almost fifteen thousand animals!

Almost as suddenly as it had come, the caribou herd was gone from the landscape. No matter how vast the herd, it was no match for the vast environment. Now and then a straggler passed by. The lone animals were as driven on their solitary trek as the great herd had been in its mass movement.

With the caribou gone, the land felt strangely quiet and desolate. The silence was such a contrast to the noise and commotion of the thundering herd of animals. If it were not for the thousands of hoof prints on the land and for the mat of caribou hair floating on the water, we might have wondered if the migration had been a dream.

"That was incredible. I can't believe we set up camp right beside the migration route!" Sally said. We sat on the beach, too overwhelmed to do more than marvel at the scene we had witnessed.

As Sally and I headed down the river the next morning, we still felt exhilarated from watching the caribou migration. This part of the Thelon River was our favourite so far; not only had we seen many animals, but there were enough rapids to keep the paddling interesting. The scenery also changed with every curve of the river, from sparse groves of trees, to flower-filled meadows, to cobble beaches.

A few days later, the river began to narrow. Between steep banks, the river tumbled over smooth rocks, and we experienced a sense of closed-in speed that we had not felt on the river before. Reference points along the shore became a blur of fast-forward motion. I kept my eyes riveted on the water directly in front of us, paddling, prying, drawing as the river swept us eastward.

Shortly after the river narrowed, the Thelon turned sharply and a rapid formed, creating standing waves more than a metre high. We stopped to check out the route ahead.

On scouting the river, we saw a rock jutting out just below the rapids, waiting to devour any passing canoe. We were weary of portaging our gear, but it looked like a short carry past the canoe-eating rock was in order.

Even though the portage was only a short one, we didn't make much progress that day—too many diversions took us away from paddling. We stopped at five o'clock to climb to the top of the bluffs, and then again at six to photograph a herd of muskoxen. At seven we climbed to the crest of another hill. Until now, there had been few hills of any size and we were lured to the top to enjoy the view.

At the highest point we came across old Inuit tent rings. Large moss-covered boulders were arranged in three-metre-wide circles outlining where caribou-skin tents had once been placed. We wondered why the Inuit had camped in such an exposed place; we always spent considerable time finding hollows protected from the wind.

On walking back to the canoe, Sally and I heard a slight rumbling sound like distant thunder. As the noise became louder, we realized it was the pounding of hoofs on the shore and the splashing of water; caribou were crossing the river at a narrow section, just upriver from us. Several hundred animals were spilling down the hills, swimming across the river, then continuing southward.

Now I understood why the Inuit had pitched their tents on the highest point—to increase their chances of seeing caribou. From the top of the hill, we could have seen the herd approaching. As we stood looking out over the empty tundra, the importance of spotting caribou became clear. Other than hordes of mosquitoes and black flies, caribou were the only living things we had seen in abundance in this vast land. To miss the caribou migration would have meant almost certain starvation for the Inuit.

Sally and I continued down the river until late evening, eager to reach the first of a series of large lakes. As we neared Beverly Lake, the scene expanded from the closed-in river valley to a limitless expanse. The sight of the open Barrens was awe-inspiring.

"No more portages!" Sally cheered, raising her paddle high in the air as the river's current washed us into Beverly Lake.

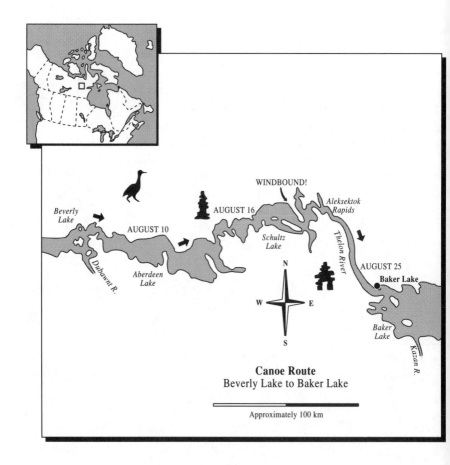

WINDBOUND!

Beverly Lake

AUGUST 10

AUGUST 16

Schultz Lake

Aleksektok Rapids

Aberdeen Lake

Dubawnt R.

Thelon River

N

W   E

S

AUGUST 25

Baker Lake

Baker Lake

Kazan R.

Canoe Route
Beverly Lake to Baker Lake

Approximately 100 km

FOUR

Lake Country

As wind-tossed waves buffeted the canoe, we settled into the steady paddling rhythm necessary to canoe the length of Beverly Lake. Over and over, our blades entered the water at the same moment, then swept back together. Sally paused while I did a J-stroke to keep the canoe tracking straight. Then our paddles arced forward with a spray of drops and re-entered the water in unison.

To measure our progress, we picked out an object on the shoreline ahead, paddled to it, then picked out the next object, then the next. After three hours of canoeing, Sally rested her paddle on the deck.

"I could swear that we're no closer to that point of land than we were when we started," she said, massaging her neck muscles.

After four weeks of paddling with the help of the boisterous river current, it would take some time to get used to this slower rhythm of paddling. We would have lots of time though. Most of the next 350 kilometres to our resupply point at Baker Lake would be across three huge lakes.

The steady, repetitive motions of canoeing let our

thoughts drift. Often an hour passed with little more said than a quiet "change" when one of us wanted to change paddling sides. We were each in our own world, lulled by the rhythm of strokes, drawn into our own thoughts.

With the lack of things to focus on came a new freedom: the freedom to daydream, to live without the artificial restraints of the city life we had left behind. We were now totally immersed in our wilderness existence. Our life had become attuned to the natural rhythm of sunrise and sunset, and our goals extended only as far as the end of each day. Sally's diary entry for August 10 tells of her reflections:

> We've been on the Barrens for more than a month now, and I've discovered that I enjoy the challenges that this land presents. I wasn't sure if I would have the stamina, the inner strength, to keep going, even in the wind, the rain, and the long days of paddling. Now I know that I do. In learning about the north, perhaps we're learning about ourselves as well.

Beverly Lake had been impressive; the seventy-kilometre expanse of Aberdeen Lake was overwhelming. The opposite shore was so far away that water, land, and sky merged into one blue-grey haze.

Day after day, we paddled down the lake, hardly seeming to get closer to the end. Many days, the north wind swept across the Barrens. Whitecaps on the lake forced us to follow the contour of the shoreline. Each night, we had to haul large boulders to our campsite and place them in a ring around the tent, one on each peg, to keep the wind from blowing our small shelter across the tundra.

After two weeks on the big lakes, the monotony of the steady, unbroken, all-day paddling began to wear us down. In comparison, our days of working together to manoeuvre the canoe through wild water or line the canoe down dangerous rapids had caused no great problems. It was the drudgery of paddling all day against a steady wind that wore our patience thin.

"Do you want to stop here for lunch?" Sally asked one afternoon.

"No thanks," I replied and continued paddling. A few minutes later, I noticed that Sally wasn't paddling hard and that her strokes were erratic.

"What's the matter?"

"Nothing." Her tone suggested clearly that something *was* the matter.

"Did you want to stop there for lunch?" I asked after more silence.

"Yes."

"Well, why didn't you just say so," I said, clipping my words in irritation, "instead of asking what I wanted to do?"

It was difficult to talk to each other when the wind whipped the words away or the splash of waves changed simple conversation into a shouting match. We stopped on shore for a rest and a chance to talk. Sally and I both knew it was foolish to argue with the only other person within two or three hundred kilometres. But sometimes, when our progress slowed to a crawl, we inadvertently took out our frustrations on each other.

Fortunately the wind wasn't always against us. The next morning Sally woke early and poked her head out of the tent for the morning weather check.

"Looks good," Sally said as she dressed and slipped out of the tent. Sally was usually up first because she enjoyed the opportunity for time alone. Often she wandered across the tundra with paper and pencils to sketch nesting birds or whatever else caught her eye.

Sally's call of "Coffee's on!" roused me from my sleep a while later. That was my cue to crawl out of the sleeping bag and begin packing up. I unzipped the sleeping bags and jammed them into stuff sacks, which had been our pillows for the night. As I rolled up the Therm-a-rest sleeping mats, Sally called again.

"Surf's up!"

"What time is it?" I wondered why she was up when the sun was still low in the sky.

Sally's reply was lost in the sound of rattling pots. When I finally crawled out of the tent, she informed me it was not quite five o'clock, but she wanted an early start.

"You wouldn't have got out of bed if I'd told you the time," Sally said, grinning. She was right!

There were large rolling waves going our way; it looked like a good day for travelling. We surfed on the crest of the waves, whooping and hollering as they carried us down the lake. As part of our preparations for the trip, we'd had a kayak rudder installed on the canoe. Instead of struggling against the waves to steer the canoe with my paddle, I could control the rudder with a bar at my feet. Not only did the rudder keep us on course, it also stabilized the canoe in the rough water. We made terrific progress, easily exceeding our daily goal of twenty kilometres.

By evening the wind had ceased entirely, and the lake became still and serene.

"Let's keep paddling," I urged, eager to keep going while the conditions were ideal. Towards ten o'clock, the sky was streaked with sunset reds and scarlets. As the sun dipped, the world became two colours: the sky and calm water were painted a brilliant orange, and the hills were silhouetted black against the fiery sky.

The stillness was enchanting. Our conversation became hushed as we drifted down Aberdeen Lake. We heard only the soft swirl of water as the bow pushed through the lake, the drip of water off our paddles, and the occasional plop of a fish surfacing to feed. The canoe seemed suspended between day and night as we paddled through the twilight. Yawns finally broke the spell and we set up camp just after midnight. It was mid-August, and for the first time we had to use our flashlights.

To our delight, we woke to another calm day. The warm breeze wafted a blend of scents through the screen door of our tent—a hint of sun-warmed blueberries and flowers and musty earth. The stillness of the morning was broken by the haunting wail of Arctic loons calling across the lake. From the distance came a cacophony of honking as snow geese rose from a pond.

As Sally and I packed up camp, we heard a strange, raspy

croaking sound. When it became louder, I looked up and saw a pair of large brown birds.

"Sandhill cranes!" Sally reported, after consulting her bird book. They were ungainly-looking birds and their flight was heavy and slow. Their long necks stretched forward and long skinny legs trailed behind. Every few seconds, their wings dropped heavily in a downward swoop, as if the birds found it too difficult to hold their wings in the gliding position.

When the cranes landed nearby, they were transformed into graceful creatures. The two birds faced each other and strutted back and forth with light steps. Then they spread their wings and took turns jumping into the air and landing lightly. During this strange ritual, their staccato calls reverberated across the land.

"Seems a bit late in the season for a courtship dance," I observed.

"It's never too late in the season," Sally said, smiling and putting her arms around me.

The echo of other cranes calling accompanied us as we continued paddling down the lake. Their raspy croaks, unadorned and simple, seemed to reflect the essence of the tundra.

The flat horizon of the barren landscape was broken by a single tall pillar at the end of Aberdeen Lake. It lured us on for hour after hour, yet we never seemed to draw any closer. By late afternoon we finally stood at the base of a tall sentinel of stone called an inukshuk, which had been built by Inuit hunters many generations ago. Thick moss on the rocks suggested that the pillar was very old. I wondered about the purpose of this three-metre-tall inukshuk.

"It must have been built as a directional marker," Sally thought out loud as she looked at the map. The inukshuk had certainly been the focus of our attention for most of the afternoon. It had guided us directly to a narrow channel of water that led to Schultz Lake.

That night, we camped beside another inukshuk. Nearby, we discovered old tent rings. As the moon crested over the horizon, the inukshuk was silhouetted in the silver light, casting a shadow across a ring of boulders. Perhaps hundreds of years ago someone had stood in this very place watching the moon rise behind this inukshuk. Standing in the ring of boulders, I felt a strong sense of history. Each tent ring told a story of an Inuit family that had passed long ago. It seemed appropriate that we also left a tent ring of boulders as a sign of our passing.

By late the next afternoon, the sky darkened as masses of scudding, rain-filled clouds passed low overhead. We saw the stark outline of cranes strutting along the ridge, but they were strangely mute. Less than an hour later, wind and rain swept across the tundra. With the rain beating down on us, we set up camp in record time.

By the time we had the tent set up, the lake had become a seething cauldron of storm-tossed whitecaps. Even though we had come north with the best of canoes and equipment, there was no way we could travel in these conditions.

We remained confined to the tent, dodging socks, gloves, and boot insoles that were drying on a cord stretched across the ceiling. Sally lay on her back reading, when a gust of wind shook the tent and a pair of wet socks of questionable cleanliness plopped onto her face.

"That's disgusting!" Sally said, groaning. Just as Sally was about to toss the socks onto my side of the tent, I volunteered to hang them outside to rinse in the rain.

The first day of the storm had been a pleasant change from paddling, but by the second day, Sally and I were beginning to suffer from "tent fever."

"How about another game of crib?" Sally asked listlessly after she had spent fifteen minutes looking out the door at the downpour.

"Okay, loser tightens the guy lines, checks the canoe, and gets water for tea!"

With such high stakes it was a spirited game. Luckily for me, Sally lost. After doing the chores at a run, she dived back into the tent, water dripping from her sou'wester. She evened the score by shaking her wet hat and jacket over me.

An inukshuk

A lone sentinel

Our loaded canoe

The next morning was still windy, but the rain had stopped. We felt restless and ready to move on.

"Beats sitting in the tent," Sally commented as we paddled into the wind on Schultz Lake.

The weather controlled the mood of the Barrens. On calm sunset evenings, it had seemed benevolent, magical. On stormy days, the weather was a tempestuous opponent. This day, the brisk wind was invigorating, and we enjoyed swinging the paddles again after our enforced rest.

At the end of Schultz Lake, the Thelon River continued its journey to the sea. We saw several inukshuks on the crest of a hill: stone sentinels silently watching our progress. These were different from the pillars we had seen earlier. With great care, rocks had been balanced, one on top of the other, to form a figure, each with limbs, a body, and a head. *Inukshuk* is an Inuit word that literally translated means "in the shape of a person." These stone figures certainly looked like people.

The strong current of the Thelon River carried us towards Baker Lake, a settlement at the west end of the lake of the same name. For nearly two months, we had experienced the Barren Lands—the mosquitoes, the caribou, the wind. Along the way, we had learned something of the history. Now we looked forward to meeting the descendants of the Inuit who had built the inukshuks.

Baker Lake Stopover

Sally and I were taking a riverside break when we heard a dull, muffled thrum echo across the land. Minutes later, a wooden freighter canoe powered by a sputtering outboard motor pulled up to the shore where we had stopped.

An Inuit man, small and wiry, leapt out of the canoe and pulled it ashore. He wore a colourful woven toque and a homemade parka, its hood and cuffs trimmed with wolf fur. His thick blue socks, embroidered with intricate designs, were folded over the top of his rubber boots.

He leaned back against the freighter canoe, fished out a cigarette from inside his jacket, and gave us a shy grin.

"Hi to you," he said. "Where are you coming from?"

"Where the river begins," I answered. "We've been paddling for almost two months."

"Oh," he said, then blew a plume of smoke and paused reflectively. "Long ways."

Without any further conversation, our visitor began to assemble a Coleman stove. He laid out tea, cookies, a loaf of bread, and a tin of meat on the deck of his boat.

"You can eat some," he urged when we shifted awkwardly

47

from foot to foot. Sally and I both felt a bit tongue-tied; he was the first person we had seen in almost two months.

We learned that Ootek was from Baker Lake, out hunting for caribou along the river's edge. Ootek stopped for a long tea break and I took the opportunity to ask him about some stone structures we had seen in the area. They looked like tiny houses with walls and roofs made of stone. One was missing a wall and Sally had crawled into it; the space was barely large enough for her to crouch in.

"In the old days," Ootek explained, "people used to store meat in them."

Then we asked about a row of inukshuks we had seen on the river. Many of the boulders were enormous and it must have taken the combined effort of several people to lift them into place. Near the inukshuks we had noticed some low walls, which were just the right size for a person to hide behind.

Ootek told us that hunters rubbed moss in their hands and put the moss on each pillar so that the approaching caribou would smell the human scent. As a result, the caribou would avoid these pillars and detour to where the hunters were hiding. The hunters hiding behind the low walls could then kill the caribou with arrows.

After his tea break, Ootek stood up and packed his stove away.

"Well, see you," he said, pushing his boat into the river. With that he gave the outboard a few tugs, and roared away.

Soon after the sound of his motor had died away, Sally and I continued down the river, wondering whether we'd meet up with Ootek again. By late afternoon, the river had carried us into Baker Lake. Not far away, the hamlet of Baker Lake stretched along the north shore. The sound of howling dogs echoed across the water.

"That sounds like a fine welcome," Sally said, picking up her paddling tempo.

From our vantage point in the canoe, we surveyed the shoreline. Rows of snowmobiles and ice-fishing shacks lined the shore, and dozens of freighter canoes were pulled up onto the beach. In between boats and snowmobiles, several weather-worn canvas tents dotted the shore. Up ahead, we saw a long sandy beach that looked like an ideal place to camp.

We pitched our tent with help from a group of Inuit boys who appeared as soon as we landed. All were dressed alike: knee-high rubber boots, jeans, nylon jackets, and baseball caps. Two boys jumped into the canoe, keen to try our paddles and *kajak*, as they called our canoe.

Sally and I engaged in animated, if disjointed, conversation with the children. They fired endless questions at us: Where are you from? How long were you canoeing? Can we come in your tent? What did you eat? When they asked if we spoke Inuktitut, Sally replied with one of the phrases she had learned from a workbook. The boys burst into laughter. So much for our Inuktitut!

"We'll teach you words," one boy volunteered.

"What kind of words?" I asked, studying his mischievous grin.

He rattled off a string of Inuktitut words and the rest of the boys laughed uncontrollably, egging each other on. I looked at Sally and winked, and then repeated one of the words. The children collapsed on the ground in hysterics. It wasn't hard to guess the type of words he was trying to teach us.

As soon as we had set up camp, I changed clothes, putting on a shirt and pants that were only slightly less dirty. I splashed some water on my face, ran a comb through my hair, then set off to find a telephone, escorted by the troop of boys. Although the hamlet of Baker Lake was thousands of kilometres from the nearest telephone operator, I reached Braden-Burry Expediting in Yellowknife via satellite communication. It was reassuring to hear a friendly voice at the other end of the line. We had left our year's supply of food and equipment in Yellowknife, and our contact, Gord Stewart, would ship boxes to us when we phoned him throughout the year.

"Will do. No problem!" Gord replied when I asked him to

rush our boxes of food and warmer clothing to Baker Lake. Gord sounded unfazed by my requests for items ranging from camera batteries, to map sealant, to fibreglass repair material.

"I'll get them on the next plane coming your way. Let's see; it's August twenty-fifth. There should be a flight this week," he said cheerfully.

Sally and I spent the following day exploring the hamlet, accompanied by a group of children. I felt like the Pied Piper as more children joined our entourage, eager to act as tour guides.

Baker Lake had a sprawling, informal feeling. It was an intriguing mix of traditional and modern ways of life. Caribou skins were pegged out to dry in front of cedar-sided houses. Many clotheslines were draped not with laundry, but with skins from caribou legs. Long handmade sleds were parked beside snowmobiles and four-wheel all-terrain vehicles called ATVs.

An Inuit mother sped by on an ATV. She wore mirror sunglasses, and two long, black braids of hair flowed out from under her helmet. On her back, nestled in the pouch of her traditional-style parka, was a young child, his fur-rimmed face peering over her shoulder.

The straight rows of houses along the waterfront looked similar in many ways to homes found in small rural communities in southern Canada. There was a notable difference, however. We were puzzled to see that all the buildings, even those far from the lake, were perched above the ground on short stilts. Later we were told that the buildings were raised in order to prevent their warmth from melting the permafrost under the soil. If the permafrost melted, the houses would gradually sink into the ground.

In the centre of Baker Lake was a Northern store and the Sanavik Co-op store with a post office. The children pointed out their school, the nursing station, and the community centre, each featuring signs written in English letters and Inuktitut symbols. The tallest structure in the hamlet was the steeple on the Anglican church.

We were intrigued by this small community, which was so far from any other settlement. At the west end of the hamlet was the airport with a short gravel runway. At the east end, we came across a diesel power station and holding tanks for the year's supply of diesel fuel, heating oil, and gasoline. The dirt road ended abruptly at the last house; beyond that was nothing but lakes and tundra. The few pickup trucks we saw rattling down the dirt road had been brought in by barge.

After exploring the hamlet, we visited Henry and Margaret Ford, two locals who had seen us wandering around and invited us to drop in any time. Henry had grown up in the area with his Inuit mother and white father, and had recently returned here to retire. Their cozy house had a constant stream of visitors stopping by to chat.

Between visitors, we told Henry about our plans to canoe to the hamlet of Chesterfield Inlet on Hudson Bay, and then travel by dog team along the coast. Unlike many people we had talked to before we left Vancouver, he didn't dwell on what we didn't know. Instead, he talked about how we could learn the skills we needed. Henry also spoke animatedly of throat singers, carvers, drum dancers, and many other traditional activities in the community. He even volunteered to introduce us to elders he knew.

"There's about twelve hundred friendly people here," Henry continued, when we asked him more about Baker Lake.

"That's about the population of a large high school down south," Sally commented.

"Well, it's a big community by northern standards!" Henry said. "I'm sure I could find an Inuit family for you to stay with for the winter."

"Thanks. That's a wonderful offer," I said. "But I think we should continue to Chesterfield Inlet before the ice comes."

Moving on was a tough decision, one that Sally and I had already discussed. Baker Lake sounded like a great place to spend the winter, but there was only one way to get our canoe to the coast for next summer—we had to paddle it there.

"Well, maybe you'll come back anyway," Henry said.

Sally and I spent a couple of days sorting out our gear and preparing for the next leg of our trip. We stocked up with supplies, purchasing bread, soup, and beans to keep us going until our shipment of food arrived.

After shopping, we decided to check out the local dog teams, just in case there were no dogs available when we got to Chesterfield Inlet.

"That's close enough," Sally said nervously when we found a team that looked like it might be suitable. We had already discovered that Huskies are excitable by nature, and the barking, snarling creatures kept us at a respectful distance.

A passerby directed us to the team owner's house. After knocking on the door, we stood there awkwardly, feeling like outsiders intruding into an Inuit home. When the door opened, an old woman waved us inside. She smiled as she pointed to a pot of tea and a pan of bannock on the stove. Several mugs sat nearby, and we helped ourselves.

When the woman responded to my questions with sign language and Inuktitut, we realized she spoke no English. She shrugged her shoulders and smiled, putting us at ease, and then left the room. A young man who spoke English returned with the woman. We learned that his father owned the dogs, but the man would not be willing to part with them.

We headed to another dog team owner's house and were welcomed with the same friendly gestures.

As we left the third house, Sally patted her stomach and commented, "Well, we haven't found a team yet, but I'm stuffed with bannock and tea."

Sally and I continued our quest, but no one we talked to was willing to sell a dog team. However, we did learn that the Inuit living along the coast had traditionally used large teams of Huskies. Many people suggested we would have a good chance of finding dogs in the coastal community of Chesterfield Inlet. Although we liked it here, we had to find dogs before we could settle down for the winter.

Our supplies arrived on the weekly freight plane, the cardboard boxes slightly battered but intact. We repacked the bags of food we had so carefully prepared in Vancouver months earlier, restraining ourselves from eating the next month's supply of fruit cake and chocolate. Finally, everything was packed into the waterproof canoe bags.

"On to Chesterfield Inlet!" Sally said as we started to take down the tent.

Just as we had finished packing our canoe, Ootek dropped by to chat. When I told him that we were continuing on to Chesterfield Inlet, he studied our canoe then looked down the lake.

"The winds pick up any time now," he mentioned, not expressing any judgement, but an unvarnished fact.

"Pick up? I thought they were pretty wild already."

"Wait till September," was his only response.

A brisk breeze pushed us away from the hamlet of Baker Lake. Like the other large lakes we had paddled, Baker Lake was an immense body of water. It was almost ninety kilometres long, and the opposite shore was not visible. Behind us, the rolling tundra stretched to infinity. After all our time on the Barrens, the landscape still looked larger-than-life.

"I don't mind the wind, as long as it's behind us," I said as we hoisted a makeshift sail fashioned from our small tarp. We made great progress. After just three days with a tail wind, we reached the end of Baker Lake.

While starting down Chesterfield Inlet, we were surprised to see the current flowing back into the lake. We were still two hundred kilometres from Hudson Bay, but the incoming tide was forcing the flow of water backwards.

By late afternoon of our second day on the inlet, the tide became so strong it felt as if we were paddling up a river. The water level rose quickly. Twice while unloading, Sally and I had to move the canoe above the lapping waves. On the lakes and the Thelon River we had rarely unloaded the canoe, except to portage. Now, unless we stopped at high tide, we had to unload the canoe and carry everything far above the high-tide line.

A fully loaded ATV!

Sailing with a strong tail wind

When Sally filled a pot with water to make tea, she paused to sip water from a mug. Her reaction surprised me.

"Yecchh!" she exclaimed, spitting out the water and spraying me in the process. "It's salty!"

We would have to camp near a creek each night and be sure to start each day with a good supply of fresh water. Canoeing the inlet also meant that we had to change the rhythm of our days to match the tide. We quickly learned that we had to take advantage of the outgoing tides if we were to make any progress at all. For six hours the next morning, the tidal current swept us along at a brisk pace. After that, progress was slow as the water flowed against us. By mid-afternoon the incoming tide forced us to camp for the day.

We pitched our tent at the end of a narrow fiord, with steep black cliffs towering above us. It was one of the most beautiful locations we'd ever camped at. Low-growing shrubs and bushes painted the landscape brilliant red, sunset orange, bronze, and vibrant gold like splashes from an artist's palette. In the hollows of drainage gulleys, the colours were especially rich. Fiery birch-filled gullies flowed down the black rock like molten lava.

By early September, the air had become crisp and frost gilded the autumn leaves. I didn't realize how cold it really was until I reached forward to brush water drops from the nylon spray deck one morning. They were frozen solid. The water temperature had also dropped considerably, and our feet were often numbed from the cold hull of the canoe.

With each day, the weather became more violent and moody. Winds gusted across the tundra without warning. Several times, we had to wait for the wind to drop before paddling.

"Ootek did say that September was the month of wind," I said one evening as we piled more rocks around the tent to hold it down. The north wind had already kept us from canoeing for two days. My journal entry for September 7 was brief and to the point: "Windy and cold. Tent-bound all day."

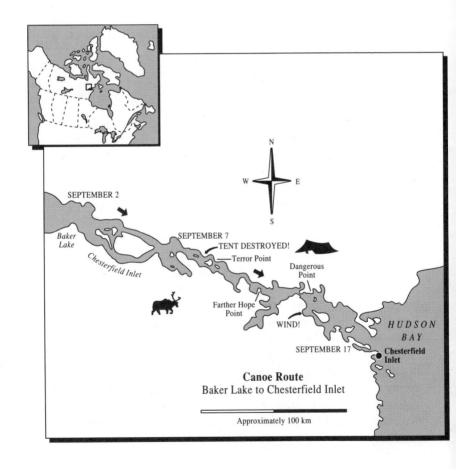

Canoe Route
Baker Lake to Chesterfield Inlet

Approximately 100 km

S I X

The North Wind

I didn't even have to open my eyes in the morning to know we weren't going anywhere. Powerful gusts of wind howled over the rock embankment and whistled around the tent. Wet, wind-driven snow spattered against the tent fabric. The nylon walls shuddered and flapped, folded inwards, and then ballooned outwards with a loud crack. The zipper pull-tabs rattled constantly.

Although this was our third day in the tent, we didn't feel rested, only tense from the constant fury surrounding us. There was no respite from the wind.

Each time Sally or I went outside, we checked the tent fly, which was faded and showed many stress marks. We had already sewn on several patches. Much of the problem was from too much sunlight through the summer—the bombardment of ultraviolet rays through each night had decomposed the nylon. I wondered how much wind-stress it could withstand.

All that day and night, high winds pummelled the tent, but it seemed to be surviving the onslaught. But as daylight filtered through the nylon the following morning, I noticed a shaft of light shining through the tent fly. There, near the top, was a tear the length of my hand.

"I'd better tape that before it rips any more," I said, crawling out of the sleeping bag. A millisecond later, the tear ripped open from the peak of the tent fly to the base. Sally and I scrambled into our clothes, almost tripping over each other in our haste, and rushed out barefoot. We tried taping the gap closed, but nothing would stick to the wet nylon.

Then, with one great, stentorian gust, the wind tore the fly to shreds. It was beyond any hope of repair.

Our tent was almost useless without the waterproof fly. In addition to keeping us dry, the fly had several guy lines that held the tent down. Less than half the pegs were attached to the inner tent, not enough for any strong wind. Frantically, we jammed the contents of the tent into stuff sacks and threw them out the door. Within a minute, we had the tent down and anchored with bags. Sally chased after one bag that was tumbling across the tundra, while I collected loose items. The gale was so strong I had trouble remaining upright.

There was a natural shelter behind a shoulder-high boulder, so we spent the next two hours extending the shelter by building rock walls on two sides. I walked across the tundra and staggered back with boulders as large as I could carry, while Sally collected nearby boulders and built the walls. Finally we collapsed behind the shelter and prepared to eat a belated breakfast.

The wind continued throughout the day. When the rain started again, we hurriedly set up the small plastic tarp that we had used previously for a cook shelter. This tarp was barely long enough for us to lie under; the peak was so low there wasn't room to sit up. We were not happy campers.

As we tried to remove our rainwear under the low shelter, one of Sally's elbows jabbed me in the side.

"Ouch!" I complained. Moments later, I unintentionally reciprocated with a knee to her back as I wriggled around the confined space.

"I hope you like sleeping under a tarp. It looks like we'll be using it for at least a week," I said as I studied our route on the map. The map gave me a sense of foreboding as I read the names of places we had to pass.

"Sounds like a rough stretch ahead. First there's Terror Point, then Peril Point, Farther Hope Point, and Dangerous Point." These names suggested the difficulties that other travellers must have encountered. Perhaps I shouldn't have read the names out loud. Sally became uncharacteristically quiet.

When the wind subsided, we continued down the inlet. Each night we anchored the tarp with six boulders and hauled forty or fifty more to place along the sides, forming a waist-high windbreak. By the time we crawled into the shelter, we were exhausted.

"Well, at least there are no mosquitoes," I said on our third night, as wind and snow whipped through the shelter. Sally responded by groaning and pulling the sleeping bag over her head.

Our bleak surroundings reflected our mood. Autumn colours had faded to dull shades of brown, and ice entrapped ponds and puddles. Even the birds, which had brightened the tundra with their calls, had departed, leaving only the ptarmigan and ravens to face the winter. By eight-thirty each evening, darkness settled over the land.

We awoke at dawn to minus four degrees Celsius and thick frost on our toques, which we had worn all night. From our knees down, the sleeping bags stuck out from under the short tarp, and our feet were chilled by the cold north wind. I looked up and saw a layer of hoarfrost on the tarp.

During the next days, the wind became our constant adversary. There were times when I wondered if it would ever stop blowing. Each night we searched for small gullies or protected hollows to pitch our tarp, but there were few to be found.

Unlike the steady all-day winds of August, the September winds came up suddenly, gusting across the water then ceasing abruptly. Even when nothing more than a gentle

Wind and waves on Chesterfield Inlet

Meagre shelter from the elements

swell rocked the canoe, there was always an air of brooding, of barely restrained violence. We canoed along the shoreline whenever we could; there was no way of predicting when a squall might strike.

One afternoon, we reached a stretch of open water and had to choose between paddling for three or four hours into a long fiord or going directly across. The wind had been calm for most of the day and it looked like we could reach the opposite shore in half an hour. We decided to cross.

We were more than halfway across when a sudden squall blasted across the water. After five minutes of high wind we began to worry: usually the wind gusted for only a minute or two then blew past. When the wind continued to build, it was obvious we had made a grave error. Already the waves were too high for us to turn around and retreat. We both knew that if a broadside wave broke over the canoe, we would capsize.

Then it began to snow. Suddenly the shoreline ahead disappeared. The wind-driven waves grew larger and larger as we paddled blindly forward. Somewhere, on a shore we couldn't see, we heard the roar of waves crashing on rocks.

When the waves first came at us, I felt adrenalin rush through my veins. I paddled harder with this new-found energy. Then came the fear, a tingling sensation stronger than the adrenalin rush. Minutes later I was in a cold sweat. I had never experienced this kind of fear before.

We were bucking waves that were now more than a metre high—four times the height of our canoe above the water-line. The wind roared in my ears. Sally shouted something, but the wind whipped her words away.

Gasping with the effort, I kept up with Sally's fast pace of forty-five paddle strokes a minute. My leg muscles were tensed against the rudder control bar as I fought to keep our canoe pointed in the right direction. Each wave that came at us wrenched the rudder left or right. I had to correct our course constantly, pushing with all my strength to overcome the force of the waves. Each wave threatened to drive the canoe sideways, and I knew it would take only one broadside wave to flip the canoe. The water was so cold and violent we wouldn't last more than a few minutes.

Nothing existed except the waves and the canoe. I focused only on my paddle, an extension of my body. I forced myself to pull with all my strength, swing forward and repeat the process again, again, and again. My waterlogged hands were numb. My wrists ached and my neck muscles were in a knot. I kept paddling, willing my body to ignore the aches of my overused muscles. Sally's irregular paddle strokes told me that I was not the only one feeling exhausted.

Each time the canoe rode up onto the crest of a wave, Sally would stretch for another stroke, only to discover air; emptiness where water should have been. The canoe paused, then plunged down into the trough. As each wave passed, it almost washed over the top of the canoe.

This was the upper limits of our abilities, both mentally and physically. Neither Sally nor I could allow our attention to waver for even a moment. We continued paddling at forty-five strokes a minute. Ten minutes. Twenty minutes. We spoke no words except "change" yelled through clenched teeth every few minutes.

Sally turned once to look at me. Determination was written on her face. Her lips were drawn tight and her eyes were wide with fear.

It went through my mind that if we swamped, it would be the end of us. I avoided looking ahead to the shore because I wasn't sure when, if ever, we might reach it. Our progress was painfully slow.

We don't usually fight the elements; those who do fight don't last long in wilderness endeavours. But this had become a fighting day. I was fighting to stay calm and not let the gravity of our situation overwhelm me; fighting to control the rudder; fighting to keep the canoe from broaching in the huge waves. Sally was fighting too. Each time a cold wave splashed over the bow, I saw her dig in harder with her paddle. She no longer had time to empty the buckets of frigid water from her spray skirt.

As the shoreline drew closer, I searched for somewhere to

land the canoe. There was nothing but sheer rock. The canoe would be dashed to pieces in the turbulent backwash.

"Where are we going to land in this?" Sally yelled.

"I'm looking!" I snapped back. Moments later I saw something.

"Over there!" I pointed to a tongue of granite jutting into the water.

We came to a crunching, grinding halt on the rocks. Sally leapt out of the canoe just as the bow struck shore, but my exit was not as well-timed. The moment I leapt out of the canoe, a wave filled my boots with icy water.

Sally and I dragged the loaded canoe across the rocks, not concerned at the moment with any damage we might do to the canoe. There was no suitable place to camp, but we had no intention of paddling any farther. The gale-force wind had chilled us right through. Our fingers were stiff and numb, cramped into the curve of the paddles.

We sat in silence for several minutes just catching our breath. Then I noticed Sally was shivering; she had caught the worst of the waves at the bow of the canoe. We had to get out of the wind. I draped the plastic tarp over Sally's shoulders and then fired up the stove to make hot tea. We huddled shoulder to shoulder with the tarp wrapped tightly around us.

After such a bad day, we had many self-doubts. The wind and waves had dwarfed our efforts. The area was so remote, so vast, and so challenging. Sally put her feelings into words.

"I gave it everything I had—I'm not sure I'll be able to cope with winter. Maybe I just don't have the right stuff," she said with a heavy sigh.

"If you don't have the right stuff, nobody has," I said, putting my damp arm around her. "It's just that your stuffing is a little wet right now. If you can handle those waves, you can handle anything."

I gave Sally a pep talk designed to cheer up me as well as her. But inwardly, I wondered if perhaps we had taken on more than we could handle. While planning the trip, we had been so full of confidence, even though many aspects of our year's adventure were unresolved. It had been easy to sketch routes and write plans on paper. Now doubts flooded my mind. Would we be able to find a dog team? Could we learn all the skills necessary to travel across the frozen land? Would our marriage be strengthened, or weakened, during the coming months?

"Well, adventure we wanted, adventure we've got," Sally mumbled after her second mug of tea. Colour was coming back to her cheeks, and the smile that I loved to see slowly crept to her lips. This was more like Sally, the cheerful partner I had travelled with across the Barrens.

I gave Sally a lingering kiss to keep her warm, then left her smiling over her mug of tea while I unpacked the canoe.

Together, we built a crude shelter of rocks and set up the tarp. If only we'd had our tent to crawl into! It had been our safe haven, a place where we didn't have to deal with the elements. Instead, we lay under the meagre shelter of the tarp looking out at the storm. Each wave that crashed heavily onto the rocks sounded like it might continue right up the shore and over our shelter. All we could see was grey—grey sky, grey rock, and grey foaming water. I fell asleep wondering if we would ever see blue skies and calm water again.

SEVEN

To the Sea and Back

I leaned out of the low tarp and saw ragged patches of blue sky visible through the grey clouds. The temperature had dropped overnight, signalling a change in the weather.

"Hey Sal, the storm's over!" I said, nudging the inert form beside me. A murmur from deep within the sleeping bag told me that it would take more than a favourable weather report to lure her out of bed.

A day later, in the calm after the storm, Sally and I continued paddling towards Hudson Bay. New snow blanketed the land, and we canoed silently through the still water.

Slowly, almost imperceptibly, the slack tide began to ebb towards the ocean. Within an hour, the outgoing tide had gained momentum and carried us down the inlet.

"No sense pushing our luck," Sally said when an afternoon breeze riffled the water. Perhaps we were being overly cautious, but we were wary of the immense power of the wind. We pulled ashore for the night.

To our great relief, the calm weather held for another two days as we paddled down the ever-widening inlet and entered Hudson Bay.

"That inlet was the longest two hundred kilometres I've ever paddled!" Sally said, when we finally reached our destination on September 17.

The canoe ground onto the beach, and we stepped out, weary, but with feelings of accomplishment after our long trip. It was nearly dark when we set up our camp on the beach in front of the hamlet called Chesterfield Inlet.

At dawn I was drawn from my sleep by a rustling noise and peered out of the sleeping bag—right into the eyes of a young Inuit boy. My gasp of surprise startled him, and in his haste to retreat, he knocked down the paddle supporting the tarp.

When I crawled out from under the collapsed tarp, I saw two Inuit men trying to suppress their laughter. I suppose it wasn't every day they found strangers camping under a piece of plastic on the beach. They came over to say hello and ask where we had come from. Meanwhile several children peeked out from boulders nearby, pointing at our tarp.

"Don't mind the kids. They're just curious about you. Not many *Qablunaaqs* visit here," one of the men said.

"What's a *Qablunaaq*?" I asked. He explained that it was an Inuktitut word to describe a person from the south. When I asked what it meant, he laughed.

"When the Inuit first met white men many years ago, they noticed their bushy eyebrows, or *qablu*, and their big stomachs, or *naaq*," he said.

"Well, I do have bushy eyebrows, but my stomach isn't big," I replied.

He shrugged and laughed. "You're still a Qablunaaq!"

When the men learned of our plans for the winter, they suggested that we visit Bernard Krako to see if he would sell us a dog team.

"He lives at house number twenty-two. Or he might be working at the powerhouse."

The hamlet of two hundred people only had about forty houses, so house number twenty-two wasn't difficult to find. Around the house were several Huskies, sleds, and harnesses.

"This must be the place," I said to Sally as we climbed the front stairs.

Bernard was quiet and soft-spoken, but as he talked, I could sense his passion for dogs and dogsledding. Over many cups of tea we learned that he would sell us a lead dog and three others because he was planning to break in a younger team.

"You can have the team in January," he said, "after I've trained my new dogs."

The dogs Bernard offered us were eastern Arctic Huskies. They were traditional working dogs—large, strong, and heavy. We were ecstatic about his offer, but confided to Bernard that we knew nothing about dogs, never mind driving a team. Anywhere else, this admission would have probably resulted in a quick withdrawal of the offer. But Bernard just shrugged his shoulders and said, "That's okay. I'll teach you."

"Things are looking up. We've not only found a team, but a driving instructor!" I said to Sally as we left Bernard's. Sally was so happy that she bounced down the road, unable to contain her pleasure.

Our next project was to find somewhere to stay for the winter. Although we had found a team here, it was difficult to find somewhere to live. Every house in the small hamlet seemed filled to capacity. As we continued looking, I couldn't help thinking back to Henry Ford's offer to teach us winter skills and find us a place to stay in Baker Lake.

"What do you think?" I asked Sally. "We can't start with the dogs until January. Perhaps we should take Henry up on his offer."

When we contacted Henry, he confirmed that he knew of an Inuit family we could stay with. He talked again of watching carvers at work, listening to drum dancers, and participating in cultural events. His enthusiasm along with a place to live were all it took to lure us back to Baker Lake.

All we had to do was find a way to get back. No one we talked to was willing to take even the largest of freighter canoes up the inlet at this time of year.

"Do you think it might have something to do with the September winds?" Sally asked, trying to keep a straight face.

We learned from the manager of the Northern store that a weekly freight plane would pass through Chesterfield Inlet on its way to Baker Lake in a few days, if the weather permitted.

"The planes are usually chock-full of cargo," he cautioned when we asked where we could book a flight. Fortunately there were two seats available on the next plane through.

Before leaving Chesterfield Inlet, we made arrangements to store our canoe and summer gear in a shed belonging to the Northern store. I looked at the scarred and scraped canoe hanging on the wall. It had taken us successfully through the first part of our journey. Our canoe would hang suspended in time, like our memories, through the winter and spring while we discovered new places. If everything worked out, we would be back in the canoe and paddling down Hudson Bay in ten months' time.

Sally and I boarded the small airplane destined for Baker Lake and found a place to sit between piles of cargo. Half the seats had been removed, and the space was stuffed with blue mail bags, boxes of food, and crates and cans of all sizes and descriptions.

During the flight, I peered down at the parallel grey eskers running across the Barrens, the ice-rimmed lakes, and the pockets of snow resting in hollows. Sally nudged me and pointed to a narrow band of water. There below us was the inlet that had given us so much trouble not long ago. From my warm seat in the aircraft, I looked down at the white-capped water.

"Looks pretty harmless from way up here, doesn't it?" I said.

Not long after, the small plane touched down on a gravel runway, sending rocks and snow flying. One bounce, then another, and we were on the ground. I could hardly believe we had arrived in Baker Lake so quickly. The direct flight between the settlements had taken only an hour and twenty minutes; our tortuous canoe route along the waterways had taken almost three weeks.

Following the example of the other two passengers, Sally and I unloaded our packs from the belly of the plane and lugged our gear across the runway. On the way, we passed several people hauling their gear towards the plane.

"Looks like it's self-serve baggage handling both ways," Sally said.

In a land with no roads to any community, airplanes are the taxis of the north. For much of the year, the only way in or out of this remote settlement was by aircraft.

Among the handful of people seeing friends off and greeting others, we recognized Henry Ford.

"Welcome back, travellers," he said warmly. "I think you'll like your new home."

Henry took us through the village, giving us a running commentary as we went.

"I guess you noticed that the Northern store now has Ski-doos by the door instead of boats," he said, waving his hand towards the row of snowmobiles. "That's the first sign of winter up here."

Our tour ended at a single-storey house, distinguished from the five others nearby by its yellow coat of paint. Like the other houses, it was raised above the ground on wooden posts. We followed Henry up the stairs, passing several caribou hides draped over the railing. As we entered the porch, I saw caribou-skin parkas, pants, and mitts hanging on pegs.

Henry walked in without knocking, but we hesitated, unsure of what we should do. Were we to follow with all our bags or should we wait to be introduced?

"Come in," Henry called. He said a few words in Inuktitut to an elderly, bent-over woman who was kneeling on the floor.

"I told her that you lived three months on the land and travelled through the area she used to travel through," Henry said. I could see she was looking at us, learning something about us as Henry continued in Inuktitut. It was a very gutteral-sounding language, with rolled *r*'s and hard *q*'s formed at the back of his mouth.

"I'd like you to meet Mamaaq Innakatsik," he said in English. Stepping forward so she wouldn't have to get up, Sally and I each shook her hand.

Then came a comfortable silence as Mamaaq smiled at us. We smiled back.

"*Teagukpin?*" she said after a minute or two.

Henry turned to us. "Help yourself to tea. Use any mug."

Tea was a strong brew. Four tea bags lay at the bottom of the pot of boiling water and remained there for the next cups. I poured the black liquid into two cups. I noticed Sally's eyes widen as she took a sip of the strong, bitter brew. That was enough to convince me to copy Mamaaq's example and add a generous amount of sugar to my cup.

During all this, Mamaaq had been kneeling on the floor. With the movements of an old woman, she rose with great effort. I stood nearby, unsure if I should help her up or if that would offend her. She shuffled to the far side of the room, then hauled a whole leg of frozen caribou meat from the depths of a freezer. Her strength surprised me. She carried the leg as though it weighed nothing and placed it on a clean piece of cardboard on the floor. Mamaaq knelt in front of the meat and waved for us to join her there. I sensed this meant we were welcome to stay.

As we sat sipping tea, I studied Mamaaq. She had shining dark brown eyes and a round face, framed by shoulder-length black hair. Although we'd been told she was seventy-five years old, her hair was just starting to turn grey.

We could not speak her language and she could not speak ours, but I learned much about her by watching. Until only a few years ago, Mamaaq had lived a nomadic life on the Barrens and her gnarled hands told of cold winters, of many skins scraped. Her bent posture was a result of heavy loads and children packed for hundreds of kilometres. Mamaaq's face was etched with wrinkles from squinting into the sun and from living many years outdoors in snowstorms and winds.

Then she laughed at something Henry said in Inuktitut. Her eyes sparkled with humour and disappeared into her cheeks. That told me more about her than anything else I had observed. It was an easy laugh and her eyes lit up as she rocked back and slapped her knees. She would be fun to stay with, I thought.

"What did you tell her?" I asked Henry.

"I said you were Qablunaaqs who wanted to be Inuks!"

EIGHT

Tiguaq

T hunk . . . thunk . . . thunk. The rhythmic chopping of Mamaaq's *ulu* filled the room. Mamaaq chopped at the frozen caribou, striking the same place with every blow until a sliver of meat curled off the haunch. The blade of her ulu was the shape of a half-moon. The handle, attached to a short stem, fitted perfectly into the palm of her hand.

As Mamaaq worked, a young man joined us and deftly cut off a chunk of meat with a large hunting knife. Holding the meat between his teeth, he swiftly sliced off a bite. I watched in amazement as the sharp blade of his knife narrowly missed his nose.

"This is Chuba, Mamaaq's adopted son," Henry said. "He can translate, so I'll leave you." Chuba was in his late teens, and like teenagers everywhere, he wore jeans, a sweatshirt, and high-top runners. Chuba nodded a greeting, then handed me his knife so I could share in the meal.

I had so much wanted to live with a traditional Inuit family, but now it sank in what this would mean—eating raw meat. I had always eaten my steaks well done. Tentatively, I cut off a small piece.

I nibbled the sliver of meat; it was layered with ice crystals that melted in my mouth. To my surprise, I enjoyed it. When it thawed, the meat was as tender as the best filet mignon. The caribou meat was not gamy as I had expected, although the flavour was hard to place; it had a delicate, subtle taste, unadorned by seasonings or tenderizer.

Crack! Mamaaq broke open a leg bone with a hatchet and extracted a piece of frozen marrow. I was hard-pressed to take my sample of the greasy, pink substance. Unlike me, Sally wasn't squeamish. She popped the marrow into her mouth and I watched carefully for a reaction.

"It's good," Sally said. "But you might find it a bit rich for your taste."

Sally eagerly helped herself to another piece of marrow, then picked up a spare ulu. Trying to copy Mamaaq, Sally hacked away at the rock-hard lump of frozen meat, cutting off ragged chunks, not slivers.

Mamaaq smiled and nodded her head in rhythm with Sally's chops.

"*Ii, ii,*" she said, which meant "yes, yes." She turned and spoke to Chuba, who translated for us.

"My mother said her house is your house. This is your home now."

She said a few more words in Inuktitut, and then laughed.

"You shouldn't be afraid of her!" he continued.

Perhaps she knew the thoughts that were going through my mind. Mamaaq must have known what it was like for Sally and me, unable to understand a new language and customs. After all, it wasn't that long ago that Mamaaq herself had been immersed in a culture different from her own, when she was moved to Baker Lake from the land.

Mamaaq rose to her feet, reached into a cupboard, and presented an ulu to Sally.

"It's for you," Chuba said. "She just finished making it."

"*Matna!*" Sally thanked her, using one of the Inuktitut words we had learned from Henry. Sally beamed with pleasure as she used her new ulu.

"Can I try it?" I asked Sally, reaching for her ulu.

Chuba laughed. "Not the ulu," he said. "That's for women. You use a hunting knife."

Mamaaq added several pieces of dried caribou meat to the pile. I wondered if this was a special feast for us or a regular late-morning snack.

"*Nipku*," she said, holding up a chunk. It was similar to beef jerky. I preferred it to the frozen meat, even though it was as tough as shoe-leather. Sally and I gnawed away at the nipku, but when Mamaaq gave us one of her almost toothless smiles, I wondered how she would manage. She pulled a large stone from behind her, placed the dry meat on it, then pounded the meat with the back end of the hatchet. When the meat had been reduced to small shreds, Mamaaq ate it.

Soon two young girls entered the house. At words from Mamaaq, they shyly shook hands. Then they quickly turned their attention to the meat. We smiled at them as they ate, but every time they caught our glance they dropped their eyes bashfully. As soon as they had finished eating, they skipped out to play with their friends.

The youngest of the two girls was Carolina, Mamaaq's eight-year-old adopted daughter. Ten-year-old Christina was Mamaaq's granddaughter. Mamaaq also looked after eighteen-month-old Matthew, another child she had adopted. She referred to her adopted children as *tiguaq*, and we learned that adoption was common within Inuit families. Mamaaq's seventy-year-old sister named Amaulik also lived here, as did Chuba, completing the extended family of six that lived in the house.

"I'll show you your room," Chuba volunteered after lunch. As we followed him down a corridor, I wondered how there could possibly be room for us with so many people living here. He paused at the first doorway. "My mom, Carolina, and Matthew sleep here," he said, stepping aside for us to see. Mattresses covered half of the floor space.

Chuba continued down the hall and opened another door.

"You can stay in this room. My mother used to carve in here, but her eyes are too old now," he said. I was relieved that no one had to vacate a room to make a place for us. We learned that Christina slept on the bed in the living room, Chuba had one bedroom, and Amaulik had another.

When we returned to the front room, Matthew was happily unravelling a ball of yarn across the floor. Mamaaq sat on the floor nearby, watching him. She smiled at Matthew's antics and didn't seem to mind that the entire floor was a tangle of red wool.

When Matthew tired of the wool and reached for one of the sewing needles, Mamaaq distracted him with a Tonka truck. Matthew pushed the truck across the floor and over my feet. Attached to the truck was a small wooden sled pulled along by a length of braided sinew. This was the "trailer," and since many snowmobiles towed one behind them, it was perfectly natural.

Each day, we met more of the family and their friends and participated in new activities. I was surprised how easily we adjusted to being with people constantly after being alone for almost three months. It was an easy transition though, because life here was slow-paced and casual.

Sally and I often accompanied Mamaaq on walks to the store or to visit neighbours.

"Can you put Matthew in the pouch?" Sally asked me one day after she had pulled the traditional, knee-length *amauti* over her head. The back of the amauti was enlarged to form a pouch, where I deposited the squirming, excited Matthew. He drew his arms in and snuggled down. His eyes became heavy as Sally rocked from foot to foot, and within minutes, the toddler was asleep. As we headed out the door, Mamaaq pulled the enlarged hood over Sally's head, completely covering Matthew to keep him warm on this crisp late-September morning.

Children are carried this way for as long as the mother, or sister, or aunt, or friend is able to pack the child. Even children as old as two are carried, unless a younger sibling takes over the pouch. Mamaaq walked much faster than usual without the weight of Matthew on her back.

When we returned from our walk, Chuba told us we were

Carolina and a friend using ulus

Sally carrying Matthew in an amauti

invited with Mamaaq to have supper at a relative's house. Just before we left, Mamaaq put her ulu and a mug into a bag and indicated that Sally should bring her ulu as well. Not yet having obtained a large hunting knife, I stuffed my trusty penknife into a pocket.

As we walked up to a bright blue plywood house, we noticed a large metal cauldron out front, propped over a roaring fire. Sally and I peered through the thick cloud of steam billowing into the cold night air and saw that the cauldron was filled with water and caribou meat.

We followed Mamaaq into the house, entering a small room jammed with people. The air was thick with the smell of bannock, strong tea, and cigarette smoke. We walked through an obstacle course of boots and stepped around children as we squeezed our way into the crowded room. The adults sat comfortably on the floor, all still wearing their parkas.

Soon after we had found a place to sit, two men struggled in with an enormous pot piled high with meat. They placed the pot on the floor in the middle of the room. The pot was quite a sight, with caribou legs and ribs poking out in all directions.

The room immediately fell quiet, except for the occasional cry from a baby. Everyone pulled out hunting knives or ulus to prepare for the feast. Many people had brought their own margarine containers to be used as bowls. Sally and I were handed plates, and someone motioned for us to help ourselves.

Using her ulu, Sally sliced a piece of meat from a bone in the pot, but Mamaaq touched her on the arm and said, "*Taku.* (Look.)" She picked up a rib, put it on Sally's plate, and then added a lump of fat. Mamaaq indicated that I should do the same.

Everyone was greasy-fingered, and we were sitting or kneeling shoulder to shoulder. The guests balanced plates of meat and pieces of bannock on their knees, the women neatly shaving slices of meat from the bones. Like Chuba, the men put chunks of meat in their mouths and sliced off bite-sized pieces. I copied this procedure, sincerely hoping I didn't slice my nose off and make a fool of myself. People helped themselves to tea or filled mugs for those who were jammed into corners and unable to move.

The room was hot and humid because of the crowd of people, the steam from the meat pot, and the boiling tea kettle. When the sweat beaded up on my face I copied others and removed my parka and rolled it up for a cushion. The room bubbled with talk and laughter. As I looked around the sparsely furnished room, I thought back to southern-style living rooms of shag carpets, plush furniture, and glass coffee tables. It would be impossible to host a feast like this in an urban living room. Where would a person cut up the caribou?

Most of the guests were older people who spoke only Inuktitut, but a young person near us acted as an interpreter. Between mouthfuls of caribou, we learned who was related to whom.

"That's my mother. Beside her is my sister. The baby in her amauti is actually the baby of that woman over there, but adopted by my mother." The more people he talked about, the more confused I became. I found it difficult to keep track of the complex family relationships.

The occasion for this feast was the birthday of a child. Until recently, Inuit children didn't have birthday parties. Instead, parents held a feast for the adults, an annual event to celebrate the birth of their child.

A woman next to me recalled the birthdays of her childhood.

"Teachers from the south said my parents were mean for not giving presents and holding a party for me," she explained to me. "They didn't understand that we have different traditions here."

She had been caught between the Inuit customs and her desire to please the white teachers, to become part of the southern ways taught in school. The teachers had insisted that the Inuit ways were backwards. It wasn't until she was much older that she became comfortable with her Inuit heritage. Feasts like this were a strong link with the past.

Although Sally and I were the only Qablunaaqs at the party, everyone made us feel welcome. Many people urged us to visit for tea.

"Any time, just walk in," one woman said. "You don't have to knock." Only Qablunaaqs, it turned out, knock on doors and wait for the occupants to answer. We left the party sure that we would have a busy winter of visiting.

The following days were filled with a mix of visiting new friends and working on projects to prepare for our winter dogsled trip. Sally had noticed people wearing thick knee-high socks that looked like they would be very warm. She asked Chuba where we could find similar socks.

"Everyone makes their own duffel socks," he said. "Maybe my mother could show you how."

Duffel socks are made from a thick, blanket-like wool material. They are usually worn inside winter boots in addition to thick socks. I was fascinated when Mamaaq sized Sally's foot by using only a length of string and the span of her hand for measurements. She picked up a pair of scissors and started cutting the material freehand, without the use of a pattern.

While Sally watched Mamaaq sew the first duffel sock, I entertained Matthew. Then it was Sally's turn to sew. She copied everything Mamaaq had done. When Sally needed help or made a mistake, Mamaaq was nearby to set her straight. Although Mamaaq spoke no English, we got along very well using sign language, our limited Inuktitut, and laughter. As Sally worked on her duffel socks, Mamaaq taught us words by picking up objects. Thread was *ivalu*, and *tiqirq* was a thimble.

"*Miqsuq*," Mamaaq said, as Sally continued sewing.

"What does that mean?" I asked Chuba. The word sounded suspiciously like one of the swearwords the boys had tried to teach me.

"It means *to sew*," he replied.

Mamaaq nodded her approval when Sally showed her the partly completed sock. We were delighted that Mamaaq was so eager to share her knowledge. She in turn seemed pleased that we wanted to learn traditional skills, to learn the Inuit ways.

"Teagukpin?" I asked Mamaaq and Sally. For this project, my contribution was to keep their mugs filled with tea and to cook bannock. I also kept them entertained. Mamaaq enjoyed my pranks, such as pretending to put ten spoons of sugar in her tea or putting my duffel socks on backwards.

Matthew had been helping by holding the yarn, but he abandoned the project when we heard a truck pull up to the house. With intense excitement, he scrambled onto a stool by the window and looked out. A man walked in, swooped Matthew into the air, and nuzzled him gently. Then he turned to me.

"*Kinauvit?* (What is your name?)" he asked.

"Ian," I answered. The man shook my hand, with a gentle once up and down. I liked this Inuit-style handshake—it was so different from the iron-grip pumping of our southern culture.

I learned that the visitor was Peter, Mamaaq's son. Peter spoke English slowly, telling us a bit about himself. Like many Inuit of his generation, Peter lived two lives. During the week he worked for the hamlet, delivering water to the houses. On weekends he returned to traditional skills of hunting and fishing.

When Peter or other people visited, we wondered why Mamaaq referred to us as Qablunaaqs instead of by our names. It was a long time before we realized that no one uses a name when referring to someone they know well. Each person was identified by their relationship with the other person. Chuba would ask if we had seen his older brother, with no mention of Peter's name. A visitor would enter and ask for her aunt, referring to Mamaaq.

As we became part of the household, we learned other quirks of communication. The family had no set mealtimes, and people ate when they were hungry. When Carolina was hungry she might say, "I wish someone would cook some bannock." Sally and I often cooked our own food that had been shipped from Yellowknife, and we usually shared our meals with the family. Carolina often looked into our pot and said, "Maybe I should have some," if she liked the smell.

The first time we asked Christina if she wanted to share a meal, she didn't answer. I was puzzled by this and asked her again. She still didn't answer but held out her bowl. I filled her bowl and repeated the question to Carolina. She didn't reply either, but I noticed that she raised her eyebrows. Then I remembered Henry telling us that children often use facial expressions to indicate yes or no. Raised eyebrows meant yes. A wrinkled nose meant no. This was an effective means of communication, except that Christina's eyebrows were hidden by her long bangs.

Sally and I had learned so much about the Inuit way of life in the two weeks we had been with the Innakatsiks. At times we had felt overwhelmed by all the new experiences, the new words, and the new customs. I wondered how the family was adjusting to having two Qablunaaqs sharing their home.

One evening, we joined the family around a leg of frozen caribou meat. I spoke a few halting words in Inuktitut, and Peter reciprocated with a few words in English. We helped ourselves to the raw meat.

"You are like my brother and sister because you eat caribou," Chuba said. "My mother now calls you her tiguaq, her adopted children."

Sally and I exchanged glances. The delighted look in her eyes told me that she felt as privileged as I did. We were part of the family.

Ice Fishing

"*Ikii!* (It's cold!)" Mamaaq said when she stuck her head out the window. As soon as the temperature dipped below minus twenty Celsius, this became the most frequent comment that we heard. It was even used as a greeting.

After a lifetime spent outdoors, the cold weather certainly wouldn't keep someone like Mamaaq at home. She handed me a jigging line and asked if we would like to come ice fishing with her.

Unable to find the Inuktitut words to express my excitement, I said "Ii," with enthusiasm as I mimed a tug-of-war with an enormous fish on my line. The pleased expression on Mamaaq's face told me that my actions had communicated what my words could not.

For the trip, Mamaaq laid out a collection of fish hooks, bannock, a bag of sugar, and an old teapot stuffed with tea bags. Sally and I eagerly pulled on our insulated, bib-style snowpants, snowboots, and down-filled parkas.

Walking at a slow but steady pace, Mamaaq led us across the tundra behind the settlement. The snow-and-grass landscape looked the same in all directions, and I wondered how Sally and I would learn to find our way across it. My unspoken question was answered when Mamaaq stopped for a rest and drew my attention to the parallel ridges of snow, formed by the northwest wind. She pointed across the lines, showing how she used them to navigate. I nodded my head to show I understood.

This was the time of year known as *ukiaq*, when the lakes freeze over and the land becomes white. It was early October and already the ponds on the tundra were topped with thick ice, so smooth and clear that we could see tiny fish scatter under our feet as we walked across the ice.

An hour from the village, we stopped at a small lake. Mamaaq crawled on her knees and elbows, using her hands to shelter her eyes as she peered through the ice. With a wiggling motion of her hand, Mamaaq indicated that she had seen fish swimming underneath.

Mamaaq picked up the chisel and began chopping a hole in the ice. Each time the chisel landed, slivers of ice burst from the hole. From time to time, the hole would fill with ice chips, and she would scoop them out with a large kitchen spoon. Deeper and deeper she dug. At last, water surged up through the hole.

Mamaaq knelt beside the hole and plopped her hook, baited with a lump of fat, into the water. Her line was attached to a handle made from a piece of caribou antler. Every few seconds, she would tease the fish by jerking the line upwards, then letting the bait sink slowly down again. We left her jigging the line and began chopping our own holes.

When a lake trout bit Mamaaq's hook, she quietly and efficiently pulled it in by winding the line hand over hand. When Sally or I caught one, we were like children. We announced the event with a whoop and leapt up. Sally's technique for landing a fish was to run backwards, pulling the line until the fish popped out. I was less flamboyant than Sally. I tried to copy Mamaaq, but my line became tangled around my wrists and elbows. I never lost a fish, but it did take me a while to land them.

After we had caught several fish, Mamaaq suggested we stop for lunch. She led us to a protected hollow among the rocks, where we could make tea over a fire. On the way, we collected plants for fuel, and Mamaaq named each plant as she picked it. We used grass, birch, willow, heather, crowberry, and moss. She even nodded when I pointed to a blueberry plant; every plant would burn.

I began filling the teapot with snow, but Mamaaq noticed this and laughed.

"*Imaq!* (Water!)" she said, pointing to the lake. I rolled my eyes and grinned with embarrassment. Of course! I should have filled the pot with water from a fishing hole; it would heat up much faster than snow.

Mamaaq placed rocks to create a three-sided windbreak before she carefully arranged a small pile of grass, dry moss, and twigs. After lighting the grass with a match, she blew gently to encourage the flickering flame. Mamaaq threw the usual handful of tea bags into the battered kettle and we waited for tea.

I enjoyed the peaceful simplicity of the moment as Mamaaq coaxed the fire. The cloud of swirling smoke and steam rising from the pot enveloped Mamaaq and lent an almost dreamlike quality to the scene. I felt transported back in time. In my mind I saw Mamaaq as she might have been decades ago, tending a small fire on the open tundra. Then, as now, she would have knelt with her legs tucked under her, her eyes watering from smoke. Mamaaq gazed across the land, a contented look on her face.

After our tea break, we returned to our fishing holes, visiting one another now and then to compare catches. Although we couldn't communicate with many words, we found a language that is universal—humour.

I crept up behind Mamaaq. Waiting until she turned her head away from her line, I tugged downwards, simulating a fish on her hook. With lightning-fast reflexes, Mamaaq pulled her line upwards.

"*Unakuluk!* (You're a naughty one!)" She laughed when she realized the tug had been from me, not a fish.

Ian and Mamaaq

Sally and Mamaaq

Mamaaq ice fishing

Later on, while I was peering into my fishing hole, Mamaaq sneaked up behind me and scared me with a "Haya!" and a jab in my ribs. When I jumped, she slapped her knees and doubled over in laughter.

Sally noticed that Mamaaq caught many more trout than I did. In fact, I wasn't having very good luck at all.

"Maybe you should talk to the fish the way Mamaaq does," Sally teased, while pulling up her fourth fish.

I put my head to my fishing hole and watched for a fish. "Ka-ka-ka-ka," I called, mimicking Mamaaq. Mamaaq chuckled, but she continued her conversation with the fish. I wondered if it could be more than a coincidence when she caught one almost immediately.

With packs loaded with fish, we wandered home in the half-light of dusk. When we neared the settlement, our pace slowed as we joined other groups. Mamaaq held her arms wide apart and laughed, and I knew she was telling a tale of the fish that got away. Fishing stories must be the same in every culture, I thought, chuckling.

For supper at home that night the whole family ate fried trout and bannock. I noticed that Mamaaq nibbled on the uncooked fish as well. Then she popped a fish eye into her mouth. I looked down while I buttered a piece of bannock, hoping that I wouldn't be offered the other eye.

Sally was more daring. She asked Chuba if she could try a fish eye. With a deft twist of his knife, he removed the eye and offered it to her. She found the eye tough to chew. After some chewing, she had just a very small, hard sphere left in her mouth, which she decided was the lens. It tasted sweet and stuck to her teeth like toffee.

I wasn't as gastronomically adventurous as Sally, who sampled everything, from well-aged raw meat to boiled caribou hoofs. She regretted this on more than one occasion, however. Her digestive system had difficulty adjusting to the different foods, and she spent many days with stomach cramps or other digestive problems.

My reticence to try new foods was put into perspective one evening when I was cooking some of our spaghetti. Mamaaq looked into the pot, stuck out her tongue, and held her stomach.

"What's wrong?" I asked Chuba.

He talked to Mamaaq. "She says your food looks like worms that dogs get from bad meat," he said, laughing. I looked into the pot, studying the spaghetti. It did look like worms.

Mamaaq ate our spaghetti anyway. Later I felt guilty when I found that the tomato sauce gave Mamaaq stomach cramps that equalled the ones we got from raw meat. She happily shared our macaroni and cheese dinners though, with no ill effects.

Sally and I went ice fishing with Mamaaq every few days. Each trip with her was a lesson in land skills, and we were eager to learn whatever she offered to teach. Mamaaq showed us the best places to find fish. We practised building fires and became more confident using snowdrifts to find our way across the land. With each trip we became less intimidated by the open tundra.

Every morning Mamaaq leaned out the window to check the weather. From the window she could see how much new ice had formed on the lake overnight. As Baker Lake gradually froze, everyone hoped for calm, windless days so that the ice could form in a smooth sheet. However, strong winds like the ones we had battled on our canoe trip continued, and the ice became uneven and buckled from wind and waves.

By mid-October the ice had crept far onto Baker Lake. Each day after school, the ice in front of the hamlet was crowded with people. We had a choice of watching hockey games, boys speeding across the ice on their bicycles, or children playing tag on skates.

"Look at me, Sally!" Carolina called as she wobbled past, wearing Peter's large skates on her small feet.

Some people walked farther out onto the lake to set fish nets. Snowmobiles roared back and forth, adding to the noise and confusion. Along the waterfront, hunters prepared sleds for winter.

The ice on Baker Lake was thick enough to travel across by the last week of October, and Peter offered to take us by snowmobile to Mamaaq's favourite fishing place. I glanced at the thermometer; it read minus twenty Celsius. With the steady wind, we knew it would be a cold day on the lake and we stuffed extra clothing into a backpack.

Peter began to pack gear onto a five-metre-long sled called a *qamutik*. The qamutik looked like a ladder laid on the ground, except that it curved upwards at the front. The runners were fashioned from two-by-six lumber. Slats of wood lashed to the runners formed the crosspieces.

"The rope lets the qamutik bend and twist," Peter explained when he saw me examining the sled. He told me that a sled built with nails would break apart on the first run.

Peter loaded the qamutik with ice chisels and scoops, three caribou skins to sit on, and a wooden box. In the box was Mamaaq's Coleman stove, the fire-blackened tea kettle, mugs, and a haunch of meat.

There were six of us on the sled, including Mamaaq, two of her friends, Chuba, Sally, and me. It was crowded, and heavy. As Peter drove the snowmobile forward, the qamutik jerked suddenly, throwing me backwards into Mamaaq. That started a domino effect as she toppled into the person behind her, and everyone else fell backwards in turn.

"Way to go," I heard Sally call from the back of the qamutik. "You almost cleared everyone off the sled!" Fortunately everyone thought it was great entertainment, and Mamaaq pushed me upright as the sled clattered across the rough ice.

I hadn't realized it would be so difficult just to sit on a qamutik. With each bump, each jolt, I almost bounced off the sled.

Great, I thought. In a few months, Sally and I are going to be dragged across the Arctic on one of these, holding onto the runners by our fingernails.

Each snowdrift tilted the sled. I tightened my grip on the lashings. With each ridge of ice, the front of the sled slammed down with a spine-jarring, tongue-biting crash. I barely had time to catch my breath before it was jolted out of my lungs with the next bump.

Occasionally a chorus of *"Yai!"* erupted when the sled tilted suddenly. As we rattled over the rough ice, I marvelled at the durability of the Inuit qamutik—and of the people who rode them. The forty-five minute ride seemed like a never-ending carnival ride. It was great fun, but my backside was tender when we finally arrived at the fishing spot.

While Sally and I helped unload the qamutik, I noticed Mamaaq move away to look for fish. She knelt down and peered through the clear ice in many places.

"Iqualuit, (Many fish,)" she declared finally.

After each person selected a spot for a fishing hole, we took turns with the chisels. It was hot work chopping with the three-metre-long pole attached to the ice chisel.

After twenty chops, I unzipped my parka. Another twenty and I threw it onto the ice, even though my beard was frosted up. Thirty thrusts with the chisel and I discarded my toque. At this rate I would be naked before I finished! I stopped counting chisel strokes, but the hole was more than a metre deep when the chisel finally broke through and water surged up.

I watched Mamaaq's friend, Amma, bait her hook and lie on a caribou hide to fish. She was a picture of perfect concentration as she looked into the lake, the fur of her hood encircling the hole. Her only movement was to jiggle the line gently.

Occasionally an Inuktitut phrase escaped from beneath one of the prone figures, its translation lost to me, but its meaning quite clear: a fish had veered away from the bait at the last second.

I noticed that Sally had copied Amma and had already started jigging her line. Following their example, I flopped onto my stomach, with my face to the fishing hole. The water was perfectly still and I could see every detail of the lake bottom. Multicoloured rocks dotted the sand, and fronds of aquatic plants fluttered in the current. I dropped my hook into the hole, disturbing the calm scene below. I was determined to catch a trout for supper.

A brown, undulating form came into view. Now I understood the importance of cutting the hole precisely to size; the fur from my parka hood covered the hole completely, preventing my shadow from spooking the fish. Little by little, the trout sidled up to my hook, which I kept moving with an even rhythm.

The trout nibbled the bait. I jerked the line upwards, but the fish had felt the metal hook. The trout was gone with a powerful flick of its tail. I could almost taste success; next time I would pull up the hook faster.

My hands and feet grew cold, but I ignored them and remained at the hole for a long time. When I tried to get up, I found myself glued in place—the fur rim around my parka had frozen to the ice. Mamaaq must have seen my plight, because I heard laughter and the shuffle of her caribou-skin boots across the ice. In my peripheral vision I saw two bare hands on my fur ruff. Slowly the heat from her hands thawed the ice enough for me to pull free.

I was surprised at how warm Mamaaq's hands were; she hadn't worn gloves all day except when riding on the qamutik. Mamaaq returned to her fishing hole, and I shivered as I watched her scoop ice out of the hole with her bare hands. She sucked the excess water off her fingers and went back to fishing.

I remembered watching Mamaaq put a handful of snow into her caribou-skin mitts before we had started out. This reinforced my vision of her being impervious to the cold. Later Sally and I learned that moisture from the snow is necessary to keep the mitts pliable. If the leather inside the mitts dries out, they become stiff and cold.

After two hours of fishing, I saw that Chuba had left his hole and was struggling with the qamutik. Together, we flipped the qamutik onto its side and propped it up with a piece of wood. Chuba draped a canvas tarp over the qamutik to serve as a windbreak, turned the storage box on its side, and put the Coleman stove inside.

Ice Fishing

While Chuba lit the stove, I filled the kettle from the nearest fishing hole. Chuba added five or six tea bags, then left the tea to come to a boil while he resumed fishing. Squatting under the tarp, I warmed my hands over the heat of the stove. I looked across the ice to Sally. She was peering into Mamaaq's hole and laughing at something Mamaaq had said. I reflected on how lucky Sally and I were to be included in the family activities. This was beyond our wildest dreams. Here we were, sharing the day-to-day life of an Inuit family.

Steam billowing from under the tarp was a signal to the others that tea was ready. Sally had made bannock for the occasion, but when I tried to take a bite, I almost broke a tooth. Sally's baked bannock was frozen solid. I copied Amma and dipped a piece of bannock into my mug of tea, but it was still too hard to bite. I had Amma and Mamaaq in stitches when I made a show of trying to break the bannock with the ice chisel.

As Amma tasted the bannock, she made a face and tossed her piece into the nearest fishing hole. She dug her own bannock out of a knapsack and left it beside the stove for everyone to help themselves. Amma's deep-fried bannock was so heavy with oil it couldn't possibly freeze.

Sally grimaced when her bannock was fed to the fish, until she tried the bannock for herself. Then she shrugged, tossed her piece into the hole, and reached for some of Amma's.

By late afternoon we had a pile of fifty grayling and lake trout. As the sunlight diminished, Sally and I helped wrap the frozen fish in caribou skins, then Peter tied the bundles to the qamutik.

The ride home in the low light was even more difficult than the morning's ride had been. Unable to anticipate the swerves or bumps, Sally and I sat tense, waiting for the next crash of the sled. The caribou skins strapped on the qamutik had done little to soften the blows in the morning. Sitting on frozen fish for the return trip was even worse.

It was nearly dark when we arrived home at four-thirty.

As we sat on the kitchen floor pulling off layers of footwear and jackets and sweaters, I watched Mamaaq. She looked as tired but as content from the day's outing as I felt. Mamaaq pulled off one caribou-skin boot; then she rested a moment while she sipped her tea. I helped pull off her second boot. I too had trouble removing my footwear—it was difficult to bend my knees in the bulky snowpants.

The pile of clothing grew into a mountain.

"I can't believe I was wearing all that and still felt cold. And it's only the end of October," Sally said. She was still shivering.

Chuba picked up her winter parka and compressed the down filling between his hands.

"Not very warm," he said. "Maybe you should dress in caribou skins like us."

Caribou Clothing

I stood with arms outstretched as Haqpi reached up and took measurements with spans of her hand. After dropping my arms, she measured from my wrist to my shoulder: three hand lengths.

"*Taima*, (I'm finished,)" she said. Haqpi then moved on to Sally. This was unlike any fitting we'd ever experienced. The clothing too would be unlike any we had ever worn. Sally and I were being sized for a complete outfit of caribou clothing, including boots, mitts, pants, and parkas.

Two weeks later, our new clothes were ready. As soon as Sally and I picked up our caribou-skin outfits, we modelled them for Mamaaq. We strutted through the kitchen, proud of our new suits of clothes. Mamaaq inspected the stitching and ran her hands across my shoulders, checking the fit. She nodded her approval. Then she stuffed a frozen fish up my back.

"Ikii!" I yelped, squirming as Mamaaq held the fish against my bare skin.

Through Chuba, Mamaaq explained that we each needed a sash to prevent wind—and frozen fish—from finding their way inside our parkas. In a cardboard box, she found a woven sash called a *tapsi*, which she tied around my waist.

After only a few minutes, I was sweltering inside my clothing.

"Let's go for a walk to test our new outfits," I suggested to Sally.

"Walk? How can I walk in all this?" asked Sally, waddling out the door like a bowlegged duck.

Only a few steps from the house, my feet shot out from under me. The new, unworn caribou-skin boots, called *kamiks*, were extremely slippery. Before she could even point at me and snicker, Sally crashed onto her own backside. We lay there, laughing so hard we couldn't get up. If Mamaaq was watching, I hoped she was entertained by our impromptu performance.

"This is going to take some getting used to," I said to Sally. We learned to shuffle our feet along the snow, the way we had seen Mamaaq shuffle when she wore kamiks.

Our new parkas were certainly warmer than our down-filled parkas. The caribou hair felt soft against our cheeks, and the fox fur around the hood helped keep the wind off our faces. Best of all, there were no buttons or zippers to freeze; we regulated our body temperature by adjusting the sashes or by pushing our hoods back.

Sally and I tested our caribou clothing several times in different weather conditions. After an outing during a snowstorm, we decided that we would be cold if we were caught in a blizzard during our dogsled trip. We needed something even warmer. The parkas we were wearing, with the caribou hair on the inside, are called *atigis*. Chuba suggested we should each have a *qulittaq* as well. This outer parka, with the fur out, is worn over the atigi.

"My mom says she could help you make your qulittaqs. She doesn't want you to be cold," Chuba said.

Mamaaq went to the outer porch and returned dragging a large caribou skin. It crinkled and crackled when Mamaaq folded it to fit through the doorway. She dropped it fur side down on the floor and sat in the middle of the hide. Curious to discover what she was going to do, we moved closer.

With her left hand, Mamaaq lifted the edge of the hide and held it tight. Using an *iqtuqhit*, a blunt-edged tool, she began to stretch the caribou skin. Mamaaq pushed hard against the taut surface, gradually removing the inner membrane of the hide. This process softened the hide and stretched it considerably.

After watching Mamaaq stretch the hide, I began working on the first of six caribou skins needed for our qulittaqs. This procedure took hours of sweat and muscle. I was not encouraged to help with the sewing, but men often helped with this strenuous job of stretching the hides. My right hand developed blisters and my muscles ached by the time I had finished only one.

When I had stretched the first hide, Mamaaq sloshed water over the leather, rolled it up, and left it to soften for a few hours. Later I continued working with the iqtuqhit on the same hide. Mamaaq filled her mouth with water and I wondered about her motives as she approached me with a gleam in her eye. Fortunately the water was destined for the hide, not me. She squirted a little at a time onto dry patches of the caribou skin as I worked.

Pushing the iqtuqhit across the wet hide, I stretched the skin even more, softening the fibres. I thought the caribou skin was ready for sewing after I had stretched it the second time. However, Mamaaq took another tool out of her sewing box.

"*Hakuut,*" she said, holding up a five-centimetre-wide blade attached to a short wooden handle. Kneeling on the floor with the hide over one knee, Mamaaq tucked the hide under the other knee to anchor it. With the hide now stretched tight, she drew the sharp instrument back and forth. This shaved off layers of leather, making the caribou skin thin and pliable.

A few minutes later, Mamaaq passed the hide over to Sally. She copied Mamaaq's every move. One scrape, two scrapes, three, *rip!* Sally gasped with shock and dropped the hakuut as though it was scorching hot.

I could tell by the flush that spread across her cheeks that Sally was horrified at the sight of the hand-length gash in the hide.

"*Namuqtuq,* (It doesn't matter,)" Mamaaq said. She showed us that it could be sewn up easily. After some practice, Sally's technique improved and she made only one more hole in the hide.

When we had prepared enough hides for the first qulittaq, Mamaaq selected the one with the thickest fur. She folded the caribou skin in half lengthwise and started to chew the hide to soften it.

While I stretched another caribou skin, Sally copied Mamaaq and concentrated on chewing.

"Pthwtt." Sally spat out a mouthful of fur, then another as she chewed the hide. It seemed impossible to avoid getting a mouthful of fur; even Mamaaq kept stopping to spit out hairs.

"By the way, Chuba mentioned to me that chewing hides is considered women's work by the Inuit," I told Sally, secretly pleased that I was spared this unappetizing task. It seemed a bit more than a coincidence that my next cup of tea had a substantial amount of caribou hair floating about in it.

After chewing a fold down the centre of the hides, Sally and Mamaaq laid my atigi on top of a hide. Mamaaq drew an outline on the leather side, leaving room for the qulittaq to fit over the atigi. She took additional measurements on the atigi using a string and the span of her hand.

Mamaaq studied the hide where the hood would be and ran her finger along an imaginary cut-line. Then, with one smooth motion, she cut one of the curves with her ulu. Mamaaq was about to make the next cut when she stopped and passed the ulu to Sally. Sally glanced first at the ulu and then at Mamaaq. Sally's wrinkled brow told me that she was worried. What if she cut it wrong? What if the ulu slipped? She made a tentative start but had trouble cutting the hide. Mamaaq showed her how to hold the ulu properly, and Sally tried again.

"*Nietna?* (Like this?)" Sally asked when she came to a difficult section.

"Ii," Mamaaq replied. I could see that she wanted to say more to Sally, but the language barrier made it impossible. Mamaaq was very patient, although she must have found it frustrating to speak to us using only simple words that we could understand.

Once the hides were cut into pieces for the qulittaq, Mamaaq brought out a strip of sinew. A week before, she had removed the tendon from the back of a caribou carcass and laid it flat to dry. Now she peeled off a few thin strands to be used as thread. Mamaaq drew a strand through her mouth to moisten it before threading the needle.

Holding the seams closed with her left hand, Mamaaq began to sew tiny stitches. Her rapid movements were smooth and efficient. Every three stitches she wrapped the thread around a finger and pulled the thread tight. A few minutes later, she handed the needle and thimble to Sally. Although Sally had always been good at sewing, she had difficulty copying Mamaaq's tiny stitches. After passing the needle awkwardly from hand to hand and trying to push it through the stiff hide, Sally handed the needle back to Mamaaq. This time she watched more carefully to see exactly how it was done.

Mamaaq sewed one side seam of the qulittaq while Sally worked on the other. Every few minutes Sally compared her stitches to Mamaaq's. When Sally had problems, she pointed to the area and asked Mamaaq if she was sewing it correctly. By the time Mamaaq had finished her side, Sally had sewn only twenty centimetres.

"I should take your mother instead of Sally on the dogsled trip. She's a better sewer!" I jokingly said to Chuba.

He repeated my comment to Mamaaq.

"Unakuluk!" Mamaaq said, waving me away. This word, meaning "you're a naughty one," had become my nickname.

Carolina sometimes watched the process of preparing the hides and she often wanted to see how the qulittaq was progressing. Like most of the children who had grown up in villages, Carolina knew little about sewing caribou skins. While elders hunted caribou and sewed skins, children learned English and computer skills in school. Reminders of the old ways surrounded them, but Christina and Carolina were often enticed away by television.

Over the next few days, many women dropped by to chat and ended up helping with the sewing. Without removing their coats, the visitors would simply sit down and pick up a needle and thread. Our qulittaqs became a group project. It wasn't unusual to see two or three pairs of hands working on one parka.

With all the help, our qulittaqs were finished within two weeks. Sally beamed with pride as she put on her new parka.

"You look like an overstuffed armchair," Sally said when I had dressed in my pants, atigi, and qulittaq. The layers of caribou were so bulky we could hardly bend our elbows. I felt like a child as Mamaaq helped put on my mitts. We had been told the qulittaqs would become more flexible with use. As I waddled out the door, I wondered just how flexible they would ever be.

Sally and I walked along the lakeshore to test our newest layer of winter clothing. Even though the mid-November temperature hovered around minus thirty-five, I was already perspiring in my fur cocoon.

After only fifteen minutes, my beard was draped with icicles and the fur rim around my parka was white with hoarfrost. My glasses were glazed with ice and almost impossible to see through.

As we walked across the lake, we saw many families checking their fish nets. We stopped to watch an elderly couple. They had chopped holes through the lake ice at each end of their submerged net. Slowly the net emerged from the water as they pulled on a rope. Removing the fish that were caught in the net with their bare hands must have been painfully cold work. Some fish were so entangled it took many minutes to free them.

Meanwhile I removed my bulky mitts and wedged them

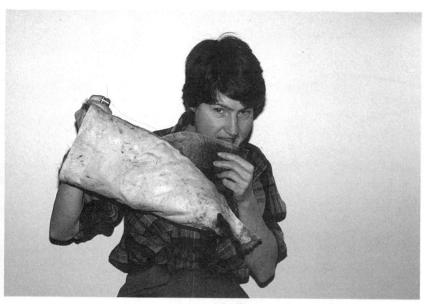

Sally preparing a caribou hide

Sally and friends in caribou clothes

between my knees while I took photographs. My fingers went numb in minutes. Photography during our dogsled trip was going to be difficult, I thought as I operated the film lever with stiff fingers.

Just as I was about to shove my throbbing fingers into warm mitts, I discovered that one mitt was missing.

"Have you seen my mitt?" I asked Sally, stuffing my cold hand up a sleeve.

We started across the lake in the direction the wind would have blown the mitt. We eventually found it half-buried by a small snowdrift where it was already filled with snow. When we returned to the fishing hole, the woman smiled and drew our attention to her mitts, which were attached to a string hung around her neck.

"That was an easy lesson; better that it happened now than on our dogsled trip," Sally said as we walked home.

Igloo Building

"*Igluliniartunga oubloumi!*" Mamaaq said, brandishing her long snow knife as she approached me. Either she'd had enough of my pranks, or she was saying something about building an igloo. Luckily it was the latter; I found out that Mamaaq was offering to teach us how to build an igloo today. It was essential for us to have this skill when travelling on the land.

Sally and I followed Mamaaq along the shoreline of Baker Lake. Here the snowdrifts were deep enough for building igloos. Mamaaq walked from one drift to another, probing the snow with her snow knife, but saying "*Nauk*" each time. The snow was unsuitable. When I copied her, I could feel my snow knife striking a layer of ice partway down.

After checking several places, Mamaaq found a drift where the snow was consistently firm, as well as deep enough to build an igloo. She drew a three-metre circle with her knife to outline the size of the igloo.

Mamaaq stood inside the circle holding the machete-like snow knife in both hands. Then, with quick slashing motions of the knife, Mamaaq cut out a block almost a metre long, half a metre deep, and ten centimetres thick. Sally and I watched closely as she cut the next block. It looked easy—a few slices with the knife along the back side and the ends, several stabs underneath, and the block broke free. After the third block, Mamaaq stepped aside to let me try.

I gripped the snow knife the way Mamaaq had and began cutting. I thought I had done quite a good job. Then I picked up the block—it sheared in two. Obviously there was more to this than I'd first thought. My second block also broke.

"*Namuqtuq*, (It doesn't matter,)" Mamaaq said. She indicated that we could use it for the top of the igloo. I tried again, this time managing to extricate a complete block, which I proudly handed to Mamaaq.

As I cut the next blocks, Mamaaq placed them around the perimeter of the circle. She trimmed the bottom of each one to make it lean inward slightly. Twelve blocks later, Mamaaq had finished the first row. Then she sliced the top of the blocks, making a gradual slope upwards from the bottom of the first block to the full height of the last block in the circle.

That done, Mamaaq traced an arc in the air, outlining the dome shape of a completed igloo. She watched me place a couple of snow blocks and nodded her approval. While I continued placing blocks, Mamaaq helped Sally cut several more. Once Mamaaq saw that Sally and I were able to work together building the igloo, she went back to the house.

"Keep 'em coming!" I said to Sally, as my confidence and the igloo grew block by block.

An hour later, I had nearly completed the second row. After lifting a block into place, I ran the snow knife underneath to make it lean inwards and fit on the one below. Then I trimmed where it touched the neighbouring snow block. Copying Mamaaq, I banged the block into place with a decisive pat of my mittened hand. The block disintegrated into several pieces.

"Maybe your blocks are too thin," I commented to Sally.

"Maybe you hit them too hard!" was her quick reply.

We went back to work, and all went well until the third

row. The blocks just wouldn't fit together the way they should have. I chopped and chopped, trying different angles, studying other blocks to figure out where I had gone wrong. I hacked at another block to test more angles, and discarded that block for another and another as I demolished each one. Nothing I did would make the blocks stay in place.

Mamaaq had been watching from the house and came to our rescue. Wielding her snow knife like an artist, she showed me how to cut the correct angle so each block would wedge against the one beside it. I studied every move, every slice of her snow knife. Meanwhile Sally supplied us with blocks and packed snow into the cracks.

By the end of the third row, the blocks were at neck height. As Mamaaq placed blocks for the next row, the igloo towered over her head and snow showered down, turning her black hair white. When only a small hole remained at the top of the igloo, Mamaaq reached up and pushed the final block through the open space. She turned the block until it lay flat and covered the opening. Stabbing upwards with her long knife, she trimmed the block until it nestled into place. Finally, snow-covered and smiling, we crawled out of the igloo.

"Come on in," I said to Sally, scrambling back into the igloo. From inside, we admired Mamaaq's handiwork.

"It's amazing," I said, secretly wondering how long it would take Sally and me to master the art of igloo building. I heard a dull thud and realized it had suddenly become darker inside the dome.

"Hey!" Sally shouted. Mamaaq had closed the doorway with a snow block, and a regular thumping suggested she was sealing it shut. I pushed the snow block out with my feet and found Mamaaq roaring with laughter, tears streaming down her cheeks.

Once we had warmed up in the house with the help of hot tea, Mamaaq brought out a shallow soapstone dish. The dish was the size of a chair seat, and it weighed as much as an entire chair.

"*Taku*, (Look,)" Mamaaq said as she pulled out tufts of

cotton grass from a small leather pouch. After working lard into the fibres with her fingers, she pressed this wick into a line along the edge of the dish. Mamaaq added a lump of lard to the dish, then set a match to the wick. Soon there was a warm flame.

"We call this a *qulliq*," said Peter, who had been watching. "It gave us heat and light in our igloos."

Mamaaq turned out the lights and we sat in a circle around the qulliq. The room was dim and I could see only the faces of Peter, Sally, and Mamaaq in the soft light from the soapstone lamp.

By tapping the wick with a knife, Mamaaq changed the height and width of the flame. She made the flame smaller so that the room grew even darker. As she tended the qulliq, Mamaaq began to hum, breathing in and out through her mouth to create different sounds. She closed her eyes and continued throat singing.

"Mmmaa, wh-ooaaa, wh-ooaaa, unngha." The sounds came from deep in her chest as she imitated the honking of geese, the howl of sled dogs, and even the sound of the wind across the open land.

We sat, spellbound, in the flickering light. For the next few minutes nothing existed but the rhythmic, breathy sounds of Mamaaq's throat singing. I felt transported to a different time, a different place. When Mamaaq stopped and opened her eyes, I saw they were moist and shining. I sensed she had been somewhere else in her memory, perhaps in an igloo many years earlier. We remained silent, staring into the light.

Mamaaq pushed the wick down so it would soak up more of the melted fat and create a larger flame. She then held her hands over the qulliq as if to warm them. She said a few words to Peter.

"You can try using the qulliq in your next igloo," he said. He told us how his family used to dry their kamiks and mitts by laying them across a latticework of string suspended over the flame.

Sally and I tried building another igloo the next day.

Igloo Building

When word got out that Mamaaq's tiguaq were building an igloo, neighbours came to watch. It wasn't the Inuit way to offer unsolicited advice, but when we needed help, all we had to do was ask.

Mamaaq's brother, Singaqti, gave Sally and me more guidance on how to cut the blocks and how to hold the snow knife. He carved the snow with the confidence and skill of someone who had built countless igloos in his lifetime. We watched closely; then he handed me the snow knife. Singaqti spoke only Inuktitut, so it was a classic Inuit learning situation: watch, then copy. There is an Inuktitut word, *iliniartuq*, which describes this traditional way of learning. It means to learn by observation and experience.

After building the igloo, we went back to Singaqti's house to warm up. When he learned that Sally and I would be spending March and April in igloos, he took something out of a drawer to show us.

It was an *ajagaak*. We learned from his son Barney that they had made it from part of the leg bone of a caribou. The hollow bone was attached by a string to a peg. Singaqti held the peg and swung the bone up; on his first try, the hollow bone slipped onto the peg. He smiled broadly and passed it to me. It had looked easy, but I swung again and again, rarely succeeding.

"After a few long days in an igloo, you'll get better," his son translated.

Singaqti had grown up on the land and had played this game since he was a child. There was a great deal of laughter as everyone in the house swung the bone up, trying to catch it on the stick. Sounds of approval erupted when Sally caught the bone on her first try.

Next Singaqti pulled a loop of string from his pocket. Sally sat beside him on the floor as he twisted the string on his fingers to form many designs. Patiently and slowly, he made one design over and over again until Sally could copy it. With this cat's cradle game called *ayarak*, he transformed the string into a tent. Seeing her confidence and interest, he showed her a wolf.

We often visited the Singaqti family to warm up on our way home after building our igloos.

"Help yourself to tea," Barney always said to us. His offer included the boiled caribou meat and fresh bannock sitting on the table.

"My father saved some caribou antlers for you," Barney said to Sally one day. On a previous visit she had mentioned she wanted to make her own jigging handle for fishing, as well as a bone game to play in our igloos.

Each time we visited, the family had something to show us. One time, they had made a game called *nugluktuq* that all of us could play. A length of antler was suspended from the ceiling with a piece of string and anchored to a chair at the other end. Barney handed Sally and me each a stick with a nail attached to the end. On a signal, four of us tried to poke our spears into a hole drilled through the middle of the antler. The prize, Singaqti announced during the game, was my new kamiks.

"I need them to keep my feet warm," I protested, and offered Sally's new mitts instead.

Fortunately Singaqti was only teasing or we would have lost the mitts *and* the kamiks.

Sally and I spent the last two weeks of November practising our igloo-building skills. Sally had mastered the art of cutting blocks, but many times I was unable to build higher than the second row. The blocks just kept tumbling inwards. I thought the problem was with the type of snow, or the size of the blocks, or perhaps the way I was using the snow knife.

"What's wrong with these blocks?" I asked in frustration one afternoon.

"They're falling down!" came Sally's helpful reply.

Our fifth igloo collapsed as we were placing the third row of blocks.

"Hmmm...good ventilation, great view," Sally said, never one to be discouraged by my disasters.

After more help from neighbours, I learned that it was important to maintain an upwards slope to the walls. Each block would then lean on the one before and stay in place.

The next igloo remained standing, but it looked more like a pyramid than a symmetrical, domed igloo.

Ten igloos later, Sally and I had more or less mastered the construction techniques, but it still took us almost three hours to build one. After a tiring day of travel, we wouldn't have the energy to spend that long building a night's shelter. We decided to buy a sturdy canvas tent like the ones Inuit travellers use for the warmer nights. We also decided to continue building igloos to improve our skills. Over the following weeks, we amused the locals with our collection of igloos dotting the lakeshore.

Our next project was to spend a few nights in an igloo to test our clothing and equipment in preparation for our three-month dogsled trip. On our first night out, Sally wriggled on her stomach through the low door.

Sally's muffled voice came from inside the igloo, "Pass in the sleeping bags." I shoved our bags and sleeping mats through the door.

"I think a bigger doorway will be my first design modification," I said as I squirmed through on my stomach, dragging a canvas bag with our stove and pots.

I stuck my snow knife horizontally into the wall, lit a candle and pressed it onto the wooden handle. The flickering flame cast a soft, warm glow against the snow blocks, making the igloo surprisingly bright and cheerful. I sealed the entrance of the igloo with a block of snow and poked a small hole in the roof for ventilation.

It was peaceful and quiet. Beneath the dome of snow, only muffled sounds reached us: the howling of Huskies, the moaning of the wind, and the swish of snow against the igloo. The circle was barely large enough for our bulky sleeping bags, but it felt cozy.

While I arranged our bedding, Sally fired up our Coleman stove to heat water for hot chocolate. Within minutes, the temperature in the igloo rose to just below freezing. It was warm compared to minus thirty Celsius outside. The snow walls began to melt, but they froze again almost immediately, sheathing the blocks in a thin film of ice. As

Ian building an igloo

Tea inside an igloo

soon as we turned off the stove, the cold crept in through cracks in the wall.

We lay in our zipped-together sleeping bags and gazed up at the spiral of blocks. I marvelled that they didn't fall down on us—especially the top blocks! When Sally blew out the candle, we noticed moonlight shining between the blocks.

The wind increased through the night and we discovered the importance of chinking the door and the walls properly. By morning, a dusting of snow covered our bags, and I watched snow sifting between several blocks. The igloo was an ice-box. Sally squirmed around trying to find a warm position, brushing even more snow from the low wall in the process.

"Not quite the romantic experience I'd hoped for," Sally mumbled through chattering teeth.

Neither of us had slept well. Our feet were numb, our noses were cold, and we huddled in the fetal position to conserve warmth. Although we had kept adding more clothes as the temperature dropped, we still had shivered all night long. Our sleeping bags were rated to minus twenty Celsius, but a rating to only zero would be more realistic! I was thankful to be learning this now, and not when travelling down the coast.

Thinking hot tea would warm us up, Sally tried to light the stove.

"I can't light it," she reported after a moment. "I've pumped sixty times, but all it does is hiss at me."

I was no more successful. We snuggled back into the sleeping bag for the little warmth it offered.

When we arrived cold and hungry back at the house, I asked Chuba about our stove. He told me that everyone replaces the rubber seal on the pump with a leather one designed for cold weather. Our pump's rubber seal had shrunk and cracked in the cold.

After our cold night, we decided that traditional Inuit blankets would be needed as well as our modern synthetic bags. Sally planned to sew two caribou-skin blankets—one for under and one for over our sleeping bags. Mamaaq used the CB radio to put out the word that we needed hides. Soon we had a big pile; we began stretching the most suitable ones for our sleeping blankets.

As Sally scraped the hides, she asked Mamaaq for help whenever she was unsure of how to continue. After helping Sally several times, Mamaaq smiled but said, "Nauk." Then she turned and said a few words to Chuba.

"My mom says that you have watched her many times. Now you should work on your own."

As Mamaaq's tiguaq, Sally was expected to learn the Inuit way. Chuba told us that when he had shot his first caribou, he was left to clean it by himself. After all, he had watched his father do it many times. Chuba added that it had taken him hours longer than his father to do the job.

With the new caribou-skin blankets, our second night out in an igloo was a warmer experience. We had made a larger, more luxurious igloo, with increased floor space and improved, windproof walls. More than three metres across at the base, our "snow suite" narrowed as the dome spiralled upwards. The back half of the igloo was carpeted by two layers of caribou-skin blankets and our sleeping bags. To the left of the door, we had dug a knee-deep cold well where the coldest air would settle during the night. On the right side, Sally had built a snow-shelf for our stove. The stove was newly fitted with a leather seal I had taken from a battered old two-burner.

Using her ulu, Sally shaved snow from the igloo walls to fill the pot, which she placed on the stove. The igloo was misty with rolling clouds of steam as the water came to a boil. After a nightcap of hot chocolate, we settled into the caribou-skin blankets.

"This is more like it," Sally said, snuggling up to me under the blankets.

"Romantic enough for you?" I whispered. The caribou fur felt luxuriously warm, and soft candlelight flickered against the igloo wall.

"Well, if we weren't wearing two layers of long underwear and thick wool pants, I'd be in seventh heaven!"

"Our lips aren't covered," I hinted, drawing Sally closer to me.

The igloo was much more comfortable than our previous one. This time we slept right through the night. In the morning, our stove lit easily and we lay under the caribou blankets as the igloo warmed up.

Over a leisurely cup of tea, Sally and I took stock of our progress. It was now early December. We had caribou-skin clothing to venture out in any weather, and blankets for the coldest nights. We had learned the art of building igloos. And after many trips with Mamaaq, we felt more at ease on the barren tundra.

"A few more igloos and a few more nights out, and we should be ready," I said, warming my hands on a mug of steaming tea.

December in Baker Lake

The front door burst open and a fur-clad figure stumbled into the room, dragging a long ladder-like object. As a blast of snow chilled the room, I went to help Peter carry the five-metre-long qamutik into the house for repairs.

"*Piqsiqtuq,*" he said, shaking snow off his fur qulittaq.

"*Ii, piqsiqtuq,*" I said, agreeing that it was quite a blizzard outside.

Pushing the table and chairs aside, Peter transformed the front room of the house into a workshop. No one seemed to mind one more project in the already busy room. Sally pulled her caribou hide out of the way to make space, and Mamaaq moved into the kitchen, where she continued sewing a pair of caribou-skin mitts. Chuba was so involved in repairing a snowmobile carburetor that he hardly noticed the commotion.

Sally and I planned to build our own qamutik when we returned to Chesterfield Inlet, so I watched with interest as Peter secured the twenty wooden crosspieces with new rope.

"Tie it like this," Peter said, pulling on the rope. The lashings had to be tied so that the sled was rigid, yet flexible enough to "give" when it slid over rough terrain. As I watched, I realized that we still had much to learn before embarking on our winter dogsled journey. I wondered what it would be like if we had to re-lash the ropes on our own qamutik at minus forty in a raging blizzard.

After the qamutik repairs were finished, I began working on a snow knife. Until now, we had been using Mamaaq's, but Sally and I each would need our own for the trip. I had bought two long steel blades, and Mamaaq sketched an outline for a handle. Then I spent the morning sawing, carving, and filing a block of wood into shape for the handle of my snow knife.

Once she approved of my handiwork, Mamaaq showed me how to make rivets to attach the wooden handle to the steel blade. The rivets were simply nails with the heads cut off. I was about to give the nail a mighty bash to flatten it into a rivet when Mamaaq jumped to her feet. She grabbed the hammer from my hand, which was poised high above my head. I watched her tap the nail gently.

"*Taima*, (It's finished,)" Mamaaq said when she had carefully made the nail into a rivet. My antics of raising the hammer every time she looked my way sent her into gales of laughter.

With my new snow knife in hand, I stood gazing out the window, wondering when the December snowstorm might end. Although blue sky showed through the blowing snow, the blizzard was still as fierce as ever on the ground.

A while later, I overheard Mamaaq talking on the CB radio. From the few Inuktitut words I knew, I could tell that she was asking about the store. For the past three days, everything in the town had been closed because of the blizzard.

"My grandmother would like you to get some sugar," Christina said to me when Mamaaq had finished talking on the radio.

Sally and I dressed in layer after layer of clothing for our expedition to the store. I didn't realize how wicked the storm was until I turned the handle of the outer door and the wind blasted the door inward, smashing it into my foot. Leaning into the wind, we shouldered our way towards the store.

"Thi...i...reall...wild!" Sally shouted, the wind whipping the words from her mouth. We had difficulty breathing as the force of the wind sucked air out of our lungs. Powerful gusts of wind sent us tripping sideways to the left, then staggering right during each lull between gusts. We couldn't see more than a couple of paces in front of our feet. To find our way, we followed power poles or patches of bare road.

We passed a few other people but we were not able to recognize any faces. The adults had pulled their parka hoods tightly around their faces and were so wrapped up in scarves that only their eyes and white-frosted eyelashes were visible. Most people wore homemade parkas, and the only way to know who was bundled up was to identify the parka.

"Hello, Amma!" we called out, recognizing her red parka with the white silhouettes of caribou sewn around the base. She waved but didn't stop to talk—it was too cold and windy. The wind howled in our ears and an eerie whistle filled the air as it buffeted the power lines.

By the time we'd fought our way back to the house, we felt as if we'd been on a test run for our upcoming expedition.

"Going to the corner store was never like this down south," I said as we struggled to close the door against the gale-force wind.

When the wind finally stopped, Sally and I headed out to practise building more igloos. As we made our way from snowdrift to snowdrift, we saw neighbours digging out. Some people dug down to their front doors; others cut tunnels straight through the drifts. We even saw igloo-shaped entrances made from blocks of snow.

Although people dug out of their houses within a few hours, it took three more days for the service trucks to make their rounds. The snowstorm and drifting snow had halted the trucks that deliver water and heating oil or collect sewage and garbage. Because of the permafrost, no sewer or water pipes could be buried underground, so each house had water and sewage tanks. Our water tank was just about empty, and the sewage tank was almost full. I didn't really mind going without a bath for a while, but I hoped the truck would make its way to the house before the sewage tank overflowed.

Soon after the storm, the supply plane came in, delayed a week by the weather. It happened to be a Wednesday, a big day at the store. On most Wednesdays, the Northern store received its air shipment of perishables—if the weather was suitable, the charter flight didn't have "technical difficulties," and the runway had been cleared of snow. Like many people in the hamlet, we timed our shopping trips to coincide with the arrival of the weekly flight. By the next day, many shelves would be empty again.

"Let's see if they have mandarin oranges for Christmas," Sally suggested as we wandered among the restocked shelves.

I still hadn't become used to the exorbitant prices for many essential groceries. The prices reflected the high cost of air freight to this remote community. Sally and I had become used to tea without milk—an easy change to make, with milk costing three times as much as it does in the south. Only the dry goods brought in by barge once a year seemed close to affordable.

"Look at this," I said to Sally. "Do you really want oranges at a dollar each?"

"I'll ask for a discount if I find some frozen ones," Sally said. She dug through the small pile of oranges. "Then again, maybe I won't. They're all frozen!"

Sally and I settled on powdered orange juice instead of mandarin oranges. We also bought a present of honey for Mamaaq.

The cashier rang through our groceries and returned my change: three two-cent candies. I was relieved it wasn't matches again. During winter especially, little cash came in and little went out of the community. The previous month, penny-change had been paid out in paper matches; I had more than I could ever use. Candies though were treats I could pass along to youngsters.

We weren't the only ones with candies to pass out to children. As Sally and I wandered back home in the fading light of early afternoon, we saw a group of twenty or thirty children gathered outside the community hall. I was just about to ask what the occasion was, when a colourfully dressed man came sliding through town on a qamutik pulled by four Huskies. As he passed the group of eager children, he tossed handfuls of candies to them.

This was Baker Lake's version of Christmas. It was *quviasukvik*, a time to be happy. During the darkest and coldest days of winter, endless festivities were planned to brighten the spirits of everyone in the village. We looked forward to a few days off, time away from building igloos and preparing for our winter trip.

Christmas was pleasantly different from the lights and glitter of the south. Duffel socks were used for stockings, and caribou antlers draped in tinsel were fitting decorations for an Arctic Christmas. With the nearest forest hundreds of kilometres away, there were no real Christmas trees and few artificial ones.

For Christmas dinner, Mamaaq laid out a selection of the best chunks of caribou and trout. Tea and bannock completed the meal. Chuba made his specialty for dessert: bannock cooked in rings like large doughnuts and sprinkled with sugar. Our contribution to the festivities was to make sugar cookies.

"What shape would you like to make your cookies?" Sally asked Christina. We had already fashioned cutouts for Carolina in the shape of an igloo and a qamutik.

"An ulu. And a tree—the kind you have in the south. I have some green sparkles I could put on it."

As we munched on sugar-sprinkled igloos and qamutiks, we joined the family to open presents. Sally and I opened gifts that our friends had made, all for our upcoming trip across the land. Singaqti had made us an ajagaak, a bone game for the long nights he knew we would be spending in igloos. Sally received a hand-knitted toque with her name in Inuktitut from Amma's daughter. Another friend had braided a colourful tapsi for me to tie around my atigi.

"Look at this!" Sally said to me as she unwrapped a present from Mamaaq.

"What is it?" The piece of carved wood looked much like a paddle used in old British private schools for discipline.

"It's a snow-beater," Sally explained. "We have to beat the snow off our caribou-skin clothes at the end of each day." These thoughtful gifts would always be a reminder of the special friends we had met in Baker Lake.

The household was bustling with activity until two in the morning. Matthew pushed a toy snowmobile up and down the hallway, and the girls played with identical dolls.

"There was only one kind of doll at the store," Peter told me later. We discovered that the lack of selection in the store had some amusing side effects—many young girls received identical dolls, and most young boys had identical toy snowmobiles. Green sleds, bright orange toques, and pink mitts were also seen in great abundance.

For the following week, the community was busy with the many celebrations of quviasukvik. Each day, during the few hours of daylight, we watched dog-team races, snowmobile races, and other outdoor contests.

During one contest, I pitted my one season of ice-chiselling skills against others who had a lifetime of practice. I came a predictable last place. Later that afternoon, Sally entered a four-way tug-of-war for women. On a signal, the contestants pulled, each trying to reach a mitt that had been placed a short distance from them. For many minutes it was an even match. One person slowly inched closer and closer to her mitt. At the last moment, Sally lunged for her own mitt and grabbed it, winning a can of campstove fuel for her efforts.

After the sun had set at two-thirty, we joined games in the community hall that lasted late into the evening. Not wanting to miss out on anything, we also attended a

A tug of war during quviasukvik

An Inuit child and her puppy

dance that continued until the wee hours in the morning.

"I feel like sleeping all day," I said to Sally late the next morning.

"But you have to get up. Today is the igloo-building contest. Maybe we'll learn something!"

We joined the crowd at the contest site and I sat on a ridge of snow, blinking blearily in the half-light of midday. All around us, men armed with snow knives were preparing for the igloo-building contest.

"Are you going to give it a try?" Sally asked.

I shook my head. "I'm saving my energy for tonight's dance," I said. Secretly, though, I was too intimidated to pit my meagre skills against these experts.

I watched the contestants search for the best snow with their snow knives, the way Mamaaq had shown me. Once each man had selected his spot, an elder measured a circle in the snow; all the igloos were to be built to this size.

With a word from the judge, the builders began. Sally and I stood in awe as one contestant cut perfect blocks faster that we had ever thought possible. It took him only a few minutes to complete the bottom circle of his igloo. Most of the builders stayed inside their domes as they expertly cut all the blocks they needed from within the circle.

We wandered from igloo to igloo, then waited expectantly near the two fastest builders. The last block was placed at the top of a dome. Then we saw Tookoomiq's snow knife slice around a block in the bottom row. With a cheer from the crowd, Tookoomiq emerged triumphantly. He had built an entire igloo in just twenty-four minutes!

"I'm glad I didn't enter that contest," I whispered to Sally. "I would have barely finished the first row by now!"

Later that evening we went to a New Year's Eve dance at the community hall. Men wore jeans and danced in boots or the duffel socks from their kamiks. Whether the women wore dresses or jeans, they all had on their best caribou or sealskin kamiks. We felt at home here with our usual clothing of Tilley pants, checkered shirts, and hiking boots.

An accordion wheezed to life with a few upbeat notes. I

tapped my feet to the music, picking up the energy as the dance began. The dancers wove back and forth, in a mix of square-dance steps and a Scottish reel.

During the second dance, someone brought out a bag of candies and tossed them by the handful across the floor. This resulted in shrieks of delight from the dancers, bystanders, and children. The music continued, but the dance was abandoned as everyone scrambled to collect the candies. I joined the skirmish, diving for a candy under a chair. Just as I was about to grab it, a hand darted out and snatched the prize.

"You're too slow," Christina said, laughing.

At the end of the dance, the doors were flung open. Dressed only in light clothing, Sally followed a group of people outside for some fresh air. Thick clouds of fog billowed in along the floor as the icy outside air mixed with the stuffy air in the hall. The mist rolling across the room reminded me of special effects for a B-grade movie. People disappeared into the mist and materialized again as it dissipated. Once everyone had cooled down, the music regained momentum.

"You should be my partner," Amma said, pulling me from my seat. Peter had already chosen Sally for his dance partner.

"I don't know how," I protested.

"You've been watching many nights; you should know," she teased.

Before I knew what was happening, I was spinning round and round to the fast pace of the accordion. From there I was lost in the spinning room—left, right, swing around, hands here, in the middle, turn with someone there. I became quite disoriented and had no idea what was happening. Fortunately Amma kept whispering, "You're going to turn with her next," or "Watch that couple—we have to copy them."

Sometimes I'd be given a gentle shove or steered in the right direction. The man and woman opposite would signal when I was to go to them. Finally it began to make sense.

The dancing continued with arm-swings, promenades, and cross-overs until the room was a whirling mass of colours, stomping feet, and twirling bodies.

As Sally and I left the community centre late that night and stepped into the icy air, we saw a group of children playing outside. A dozen boys scrambled after a chunk of ice in an improvised hockey game, puffing clouds of vapour into the air. Nearby, young girls were sliding down a snowbank.

Sally and I arrived home exhausted after dancing all night, but as soon as we opened Mamaaq's door, we knew that we were about to step into another party that might go on for hours. Mamaaq and other adults were playing cards, talking, and downing mug after mug of tea. We joined the card game; as always, laughter bridged any language or cultural gaps. The girls and Matthew were still playing their own games, but like Sally and me, they were fading fast. The card game was still going strong when we headed to our room around four in the morning.

"Here's to dogsledding and the new year," I said to Sally, raising a mug of strong, black tea. We had been too busy dancing at midnight to make a toast.

Sally clinked her mug against mine. "And to igloos that don't fall down!" she said, grinning.

A couple of mornings later, we packed the last of our gear for our flight to Chesterfield Inlet. Although we looked forward to the adventures ahead, we felt sad about leaving Mamaaq and the friends we had made in Baker Lake.

As we went to the door with Mamaaq, Sally and I felt as awkward as the day we had arrived, only for different reasons. I was unable to tell Mamaaq how much she had helped us, how much it meant to be accepted into her family, to become her tiguaq. I had memorized a long Inuktitut phrase to say thank you, but somehow the words would have been inadequate to express our thanks. With tears in her eyes, Sally gave Mamaaq a big hug.

I took some comfort that there is no Inuktitut word equivalent to the English "goodbye." It would have seemed too final.

THIRTEEN

Finding a Dog Team

The first sound that Sally and I heard as we walked from the airfield to the hamlet of Chesterfield Inlet was the howling of sled dogs. It was a wild, haunting howl that sounded more like a pack of wolves than dogs.

"Do you think that's our team?" Sally asked.

"Could be," I replied. I detected a mix of excitement and apprehension in Sally's voice. The apprehension came from Sally's childhood fear of dogs. The excitement was from the anticipation of meeting our team.

For years, we had dreamed of travelling across the Arctic by dogsled, a companionable team of Huskies fanned out before us. Now, here we were in Chesterfield Inlet to pick up a team of dogs from Bernard Krako. The next five months would be the most challenging part of our year in the north—learning how to handle a team of Huskies, then sledding for several months with the team along the coast of Hudson Bay.

Sally and I were able to find a small room to rent for the months of January and February while we trained with our team of dogs. By the time we had carried in all our gear, the room was stuffed corner to corner with sacks of dog food, boxes, and canvas bags.

"Will there be any room for us?" Sally wondered aloud, dragging the last bag of expedition gear through the door.

After settling in, we visited Bernard Krako to enquire about the team we had arranged to buy when we had passed through in September. As always in an Inuit home, several mugs of tea preceded any serious conversation.

"Do you think we could see the dogs now?" I asked, after we had chatted for a while.

"I don't have the team anymore," Bernard said, then paused for a moment. "They died."

Dead? We were stunned. In an instant, all our dreams were shattered.

Bernard never told us the whole story, but we guessed the dogs had died of distemper, a disease that claims many Huskies. The news shocked us. However, one of the traits we had admired in Mamaaq was the Inuit way of quietly accepting things as they were, and we tried to respond as she would have.

"Oh well, *quyanami*, (it can't be helped,)" I said quietly, restraining my emotions.

There was nothing to gain by being angry; that would not bring the dogs back. All we could do was begin looking for another team. Sally and I were worried. Before leaving on our trip, a dog trainer had given us some advice: the most important thing is to find a "working team" and not try to piece one together by ourselves.

Bernard gave us the names of other people in Chesterfield Inlet who had dog teams. All day long, we went from house to house. People were sympathetic, but either their dogs were not in sledding condition or they couldn't be spared. One man was willing to sell, but the dogs were not Huskies; their coats were thin and the animals lay shivering at their stakes in the snow. They would not have survived sleeping on the open, windswept sea ice.

Sally and I continued our search for dogs the next day, and the next. Increasingly discouraged, we struggled to communicate with people who spoke little English, we waited for others who were out hunting, and we tracked down the owners of stray dogs. Our efforts produced only three dogs that looked suitable for the task.

We took stock of our situation. In our room was a pile of snow anchors, stake-out chains, and other dogsledding paraphernalia. Our reference book, which we had studied until we could harness imaginary dogs in our sleep, was balanced atop the pile of dog food. The only ingredient missing, other than experience, was a team of dogs. A rather crucial element!

"Do you think we'll ever get to use this stuff?" I glumly asked Sally.

We sat in silence, staring at our pile of gear. A few minutes later, we heard the thumping of snow boots down the hall. A friend burst in.

"Good news!" he shouted. "I've found some dogs for you!"

We were like excited children as he took us to meet Eli Kimmeliarjuk. Eli was an older man, with a face burned exceptionally dark from a life of hunting. He spoke English well, but we had trouble hearing his quiet voice.

"Would you sell us some dogs?" I asked Eli. For a moment he didn't answer but studied us instead.

"No," he said quietly, then paused. "I should sell my whole team."

"How many dogs are there?" I asked, trying to contain my excitement. I wanted to jump up and let out a whoop of joy, but we still had to bargain for the dogs.

"Five dogs," he said. "It's a good team. A working team." Eli named a price that was within our budget.

Eli took us to the shore where his dogs were chained, just off the sea ice of Hudson Bay. As we walked, he told us more about them. The lead dog, Oonirgluk, was seven years old and the others were three and four—perfect ages for strenuous travel. Eli had trained them from pups, and until a few weeks ago, he had used the team every few days to take him hunting.

"I fell off the qamutik and hurt my leg. Maybe I'm too

old now," he said rather sadly. That explained why he was willing to sell the team.

As we approached, five mounds of snow exploded into jumping, happy creatures. Shaking snow from their coats, they leapt against the chain. I could see why they were called Huskies. The dogs were large and strong, standing as high as the top of my legs.

Eli's dogs were the eastern Arctic breed of Huskies, and they looked more like wolves than dogs. They had deep chests, and their paws were nearly the size of Sally's hands. Each dog stood with its ears perked forward and its long, bushy tail held up. Thick fur covered their bodies, and their stocky build suggested power rather than speed.

I started to approach the row of chained dogs, and then remembered that some dogs will bite, despite a wagging tail. Sled dogs have a reputation for viciousness. Many other teams we had looked at were made up of growling, snarling creatures that looked as if they would rather devour us than pull our sled. These dogs looked friendly, but . . .

While I debated the wisdom of offering my hand in friendship to a wolflike creature with such powerful jaws, Sally moved forward.

"Good dog. Good boy," she said softly, clucking her tongue as if the dogs were chickens. Much to my surprise, she walked up to one dog without any hesitation. Then she scratched his ears and ruffled his fur. Was this Sally? The Sally I knew and loved, with a lifelong fear of dogs?

"What's the matter? Are you afraid?" Sally asked, smothering a grin. "They won't bite."

The smallest dog, Kakpik, took to Sally as if she were a long-lost friend. From that moment to the end of our trip, so long as Sally was in sight, Kakpik's eyes were on her. Although I had joined Sally among the dogs, Kakpik hardly noticed that I was there. With one paw possessively on Sally's foot, he grinned his broad canine smile at her, tongue lolling over his teeth. Kakpik wriggled with excitement, as if his wagging tail was powering his body instead of the other way around.

Some of Eli's dogs were more eager to be patted than others, but only one was skittish, shy of our touch. As I tried to coax him over for a chin rub, another dog came up to me from the side. Before I knew what was happening, he'd lifted a leg and urinated on my boot.

"That's Oonirgluk," Eli said. "I think he likes you."

I hope he doesn't like me this much every day, I thought. I reached out to stroke him. His fur was thick, a double layer made up of a fine, woolly undercoat and a coarse dressing of long guard hairs.

With great patience, Eli repeated each dog's name. Oonirgluk was the leader. Then came Kakpik, also capable of leading. Arnako was the shy white dog. Anukti was the most playful, leaping into the air and tugging at Sally's caribou-skin coat. Finally there was Tokak, the largest of the dogs. We listened carefully, repeating the names until they sounded right.

I was ecstatic that Eli was willing to part with such a healthy, happy team of Huskies. We were now the proud owners of a working team, including the most important member, a trained lead dog. Best of all, they were all males. I had heard stories of the terrible fights among male dogs when a female came into heat.

"Great," I said to Sally. "I was hoping to avoid the kind of distractions a female would create."

"Really?" she asked, raising her eyebrows.

"Well, among the dogs, anyway," I replied quickly.

Now that we owned a team of Huskies, all we had to do was learn how to feed them, harness them, hook them up, care for them, control them, and run them. We had studied our reference book thoroughly, but now that we were in charge of a live, leaping team, I suddenly realized that we had a great deal to learn. Their lives, and ours, would eventually depend on our ability to look after them.

On our way back home we stopped at Eli's. I had hundreds of questions about the dogs but remembered that Inuit consider it impolite to be too direct. We waited until after tea to bring up the topic of feeding the dogs.

Oonirgluk and Arnako

Sally's favourite dog, Kakpik

"They're Huskies; they'll eat anything," Eli said.

I had hoped he would be more specific. After some prompting, we learned that their meal was usually a chunk of seal, caribou, or fish. When meat was scarce, he would feed them each four cups of dog food. Eli showed us how to mix dry dog food with hot water to allow the kernels to absorb water. During cold weather, he suggested we should stir in small squares of seal fat for extra energy.

"When do you give them water?" I asked.

"They don't need water. They eat snow," Eli said, shrugging his shoulders. His answer reinforced my impression that these tough creatures were well suited for travelling in the north.

Sally and I visited the dogs daily, and they quickly came to recognize us. Even when we were still a distance away, they would stand, stretch, and shake the snow off their fur. By the time we reached them, there was a row of tail-wagging, furry creatures. They always greeted us enthusiastically. I hoped this was not just because our arrival often meant it was supper time.

During the first week, we came to know the dogs better. Each dog had a distinctive character, from Oonirgluk, who was rather aloof, to Kakpik, who was so excitable he whined loudly and pawed the snow as soon as he saw us coming. Arnako, who had been so timid when we first met the team, still retreated to the end of his chain every time we approached.

In contrast to Arnako, Anukti was a mischievous and outgoing creature who chewed on our kamik laces or the back of our atigis when we weren't looking. His name meant "eater of excrement," which we discovered was appropriate. We learned to kick the frozen piles out of his reach because he had a disgusting habit of chewing on them for something to do.

"You're not licking *my* face," Sally said one afternoon, pushing away the foul-breathed Anukti when he jumped up to greet her.

The last dog on the chain was Tokak, a big, lovable dog

with floppy ears and a grizzled face. He looked unkempt, and his matted black fur was often draped with snow and ice.

While giving the dogs time to become accustomed to us, Sally and I began to prepare our equipment for sledding. Our first project was to build our qamutik. The runners were made from two-by-six fir and had high-density plastic screwed to the bottom. We lashed the sixteen crosspieces tightly, the way Peter Innakatsik had shown us. When we had finished, the qamutik was almost five metres long and seventy-five centimetres wide. I hoped it would be sturdy enough to carry Sally and me, the food, and our equipment—a load of more than three hundred kilograms.

A week after we had been introduced to the dogs, Eli finally agreed to take us out with the team.

"Maybe we could go today. They know you now," he said one morning. We had been impatient to go on our first run, but now I realized that it must have been important for the dogs to become used to us first.

Sally and I waited for Eli at the shoreline where the dogs were chained out just off the sea ice. Eli roared up a few minutes later on a snowmobile.

"I'm going hunting, but I'll help you hook up and follow you by Ski-doo for a while," Eli said.

"He's not going with us?" Sally whispered to me, a worried look on her face. "We don't have a clue what we're doing."

"It's okay. I read the musher's handbook again this morning," I whispered back. Sally only looked more worried after my words of encouragement.

I watched carefully as Eli harnessed the dogs, each one in a nylon harness of a different colour. Eli asked Sally to stretch out the lead lines for the dogs. There were five lines of different lengths, all joined to a tow rope at the front of our new qamutik. Oonirgluk was clipped onto the longest line, then the others in descending order of rank, finishing with Tokak on the shortest line.

In the eastern Arctic, people use a fan hitch, which has a

separate trace for each dog. The line for the lead dog was ten metres long, while the others were progressively shorter. This kind of hitch is preferred because it allows each dog to choose its route through the rough ice and across cracks. I had read that if a dog stumbled, it could regain its footing without being dragged along by the others.

Brimming with book knowledge, I helped Eli hook up our team. I briefly wondered if this would be like wandering into a den of lions armed only with a book on lion taming.

Eli reviewed the list of commands: a whistle to go; and a long, drawn-out "Whoa" to stop. *"Hulla"* was the command for a left turn, and *"Howa-ii"* meant a right turn. I repeated the words over and over, trying to get the correct intonation.

Eli motioned for me to sit on the front of the qamutik. Sally knelt just behind me.

"Are you ready?" Eli asked.

The dogs were definitely ready. They howled and whined, digging the snow in their excitement. The instant Eli lifted the snow hook that anchored the sled we were off. The dogs lunged against their harnesses and sprinted down the slope towards the sea ice. It was all I could do to stay on the qamutik.

They ran with the enthusiasm of dogs who had been chained up for a long time. Towering lumps of upturned ice near the shore whizzed past us like a picket fence seen from a speeding car. I clenched my fingers around the lashings, kept my toes out of the way, and watched hopefully for an opening to the smooth sea ice.

"Hulla, hulla," I yelled when we were about to crash into a large block of ice. Fortunately, the dogs turned sharply just before the obstacle. Unfortunately, the sled didn't follow the same route. We rode up the side of the ice and the sled turned onto one runner, still going fast. Sally and I were thrown from the qamutik.

I gasped a wheezing "Whoa!" as I hit the ice. Then, with a desperate lunge, I grabbed the last crosspiece of the sled as it passed me. The dogs were still running flat out; I wondered if they knew of the disaster behind them. I tried pulling myself back onto the sled, but it was impossible. My body bounced and flopped against the rough ice like a rag doll.

Desperately I yelled "WHOA!" but the dogs increased their speed, spurred on by my loud voice.

"WHOA! WHOA!" I was becoming breathless and weak. A few seconds more and I'd have to let go of the sled. Then I remembered that Eli had said the signal to stop the team should be delivered in a low, drawn-out manner.

"Whoooaaaaaa," I said. This was quite a feat while being dragged over the rough ice! The dogs slowed slightly.

I looked over my shoulder and saw Sally pick herself up. She started to run, trying to catch up. I didn't dare let go. I hung onto the sled with both hands and was dragged like a human snowplow until the dogs decided to stop on their own.

As soon as the dogs stopped, I threw the rear snow hook into the snow. The hook was a fierce-looking claw made from steel, with two sharp points that gripped the snow. The rear snow hook had been just out of reach as I was dragged behind the qamutik. For extra measure, I stamped the front hook into the snow as well to anchor the team.

"How do you like dogsledding so far?" I asked Sally when she caught up to the sled.

"I don't know. I was only on the sled for thirty seconds!"

Sally and I repositioned ourselves on the qamutik and set off again, following Eli's snowmobile tracks. Eli, who had been watching our performance, accompanied us for the first kilometre as I practised turning the team left and right. After the team responded to several of my commands, Eli continued on his trip to the edge of the ice floe, leaving us to figure things out for ourselves.

I could think of few experiences that compared with the thrill of speeding along the ice as five Huskies eagerly leaned into their harnesses. Snow from the dogs' feet flew through the air and bounced off my face while I hung on tightly to the qamutik.

"This is more like it," I called over my shoulder to Sally.

"I think we've got it!" she called back.

Suddenly the dogs lurched to the left. A stray female dog had joined us and was running ahead of the team. Naturally the five males were more interested in following her than in heeding my commands. And she had no consideration for the sled or its passengers.

Left and right we went, over clumps of ice and down into hollows, until we reached the smooth sea ice.

"Whoa," I called slowly. I threw the snow hook off the sled, causing snow to spray high over my head and directly into Sally's face. When the hook caught on a lump of ice, the qamutik jerked to an abrupt stop. Sally kept going and tumbled off the sled into the snow. Head first.

Nothing would induce the stray dog to leave. We chased her. We threw lumps of ice at her. We tried to grab her by the scruff of the neck, but she crawled under the belly of one dog after another to avoid our reach.

The dogs ran about, yapping and jumping while Sally and I slipped, cursed, and lunged at the obnoxious mutt. Our first and most important run with our new dog team was becoming a major fiasco. After several minutes, I managed to catch the dog. I dumped her onto the sled. She went limp and Sally held her down while I prepared to continue our run.

The instant the sled moved, the dog wriggled from Sally's grip and dashed in front of the team. Amazingly, we caught her again. Although I felt like throttling the loose dog, I tied her on a lead to the back of the sled. She followed at a trot and our progress was somewhat better.

This time the dogs chose a more sensible route through the jumble of sea ice. Thick slabs stuck up at forty-five degree angles, towering above us. With concern, I wondered if the ice was strong enough in the deep trenches between the uplifted blocks of ice. The ice under us creaked and groaned, adding to our worries. We had no idea if it was dangerous to be there; during our zigzag route following the female, we had lost the snowmobile trail.

The dogs dropped into a trench between house-sized

blocks and floundered in the powdery snow. The qamutik followed, slamming heavily into the trench and nearly running over the dogs before becoming stuck. Together Sally and I heaved the sled around while the dogs collapsed onto the snow and watched.

By this time, each dog was hopelessly tangled in his lead line. The five lines were woven into one short, braided tangle, leaving the dogs bunched up near the qamutik. While Sally stood on the snow hook, I untangled one line at a time, working with bare hands. The temperature was minus thirty-five, not taking into account the windchill factor.

My fingers throbbed with cold. When the pain became overwhelming, I stuffed them back into mitts and ran in circles, flapping my arms to restore circulation. This performance must have looked like play, because the dogs jumped up and tumbled in the snow, tangling their traces again.

Our book on dogsledding had emphasized that a musher should *never* yell in anger at the dogs. But when I was surrounded by a tangled mass of rope and fur for the third time in ten minutes, I did just that. This wasn't the close bonding of man and dog that I had hoped for; in fact, this trip seemed to be more of a wrestling match. Finally, with energy born of frustration and anger, I manhandled the dogs into the direction I wanted them to take.

The dogs finally sorted out, I tried to whistle to get the team going. That was Eli's signal for the dogs to start running but my lips and cheeks were too numbed to do more than send out a puff of air. The dogs simply looked at me.

We spent the next hour coaxing, pleading, and shouting directions at the dogs. I couldn't help thinking that this would make a great episode for "America's Funniest Home Videos." I'm sure the dogs suffered as much from the confusion as we did.

"Maybe they don't understand English," Sally suggested.

She had a point. My pronunciation of Eli's commands was probably not correct. No matter how hard I tried, my

"Hulla" and "Howa-ii" sounded different from his.

Eventually the dogs responded. By the time we returned to the stake-out area, two hours had passed and we had travelled less than two kilometres. Everything had gone wrong. I had lost my temper with the dogs—the worst possible way to start with a new team. I felt that the dogs would never listen to me after this poor first impression.

I was feeling beat when we began to unhook the dogs from the qamutik. As I straddled Tokak to pull the harness over his head, he reached up and gave me a sloppy, wet lick across my face. I looked over to Sally and saw her rubbing Kakpik's stomach; both looked tired but content. Each dog wagged his tail or jumped up when we approached, and we eagerly patted and praised them in turn. It was impossible to stay angry at a ball of fur with a wagging tail. And they didn't seem the least displeased with us.

That evening, Sally and I reflected on the day's events. We compared bruises and speculated about our next attempt at dogsledding.

Months earlier, a well-meaning dog trainer had listed the disasters that would befall us as novice dog mushers: dogs getting tangled, the team not obeying our commands, the qamutik flipping over, Sally and I getting lost.

"Well, all those disasters happened on our first day," Sally said wearily.

"Yeah, now that they're out of the way we can have some fun!" I replied. What else could possibly happen to us?

FOURTEEN

Working as a Team

Our first run proved that we would have no trouble getting the dogs to pull. All we had to do was get them to pull in the right direction.

I dumped a tangle of nylon harnesses onto the snow and wondered how to fit them onto each of the five leaping, yelping, hyperactive dogs. Sally and I first sorted out which harness belonged to which dog. Then I turned Oonirgluk's harness over and over in my hands, trying to figure out which way it went on. It had looked so easy when Eli harnessed the dogs.

"Do you remember how Eli put this thing on?" I asked Sally. She shook her head.

I struggled to put Oonirgluk's head through a loop of webbing before I realized the harness was upside-down. After a few more false starts, I discovered that the easiest way was to straddle the dog and slip the padded yoke over his head. Then, worried about hurting him, I gently bent one of Oonrigluk's front legs and tried to guide it into a leg loop. Like a stubborn toddler, he rolled onto his side. I was less concerned about hurting Oonrigluk as I lifted him by the harness and stuffed his other leg through the final loop. After all that, I moved on to the next dog.

Sally and I became chilled and frustrated during the hour it took to harness the dogs and sort out the lead lines. Meanwhile the wind had picked up, making visibility poor. I watched the dogs lunge against their chains; they were yapping and howling in anticipation of the run. Even the most timid dog, Arnako, was eagerly leaping into the air. It would not be fair to unharness them without a run, we decided.

While I clipped the dogs to the sled, Sally stood on the rear snow hook, anchoring it even more firmly in the snow.

"If the hook comes out, hop onto the sled and hang on!" I shouted over the din of howling dogs. Sally's response was drowned out by Kakpik's whining, but I gathered she wasn't too enthusiastic about my plan.

As soon as we pulled up the snow hooks, the dogs sprinted with a release of pent-up energy, like racehorses bursting from a starting gate. This time Sally and I were ready for the fast run down the hill. We even anticipated the sharp turns around the towering lumps of ice. But when the dogs ignored my commands and took us careening over a stretch of bumpy intertidal ice, we were almost tossed off the sled.

"This is like driving a car without a steering wheel," Sally exclaimed, wrapping her arms around me in an effort to keep her balance.

"Let go! I can't hold on," I pleaded. Sally's desperate hug had pinned my arms to my sides, and I struggled to keep my balance.

Once the dogs slowed from their initial sprint, I noticed that Oonirgluk kept looking back at me, confused about which way to go. I repeated my version of the Inuktitut commands over and over again. Many times I had to stop the team and herd the dogs in the direction I wanted. At this rate, I would spend as much time herding the dogs as sledding.

Visibility was minimal, but we could still see the sun through the swirling snow. I squinted across the sea ice looking for landmarks, then remembered Mamaaq's lesson about the parallel ridges of windblown snow. Using the ridges to give us a sense of direction, I did my best to keep the dogs running in a straight line.

After an hour, I turned the dogs in a large circle, keeping an eye on the position of the sun to find our way home. Now we had to face the wind. It whipped through our clothes and sucked the last warmth from our bodies. Sitting on the qamutik in a blizzard at minus forty was a numbing experience. Through chattering teeth, we each vowed to wear every layer of clothing we owned for the next run.

Although Sally and I couldn't see where we were going, Oonirgluk led the team back to the stake-out area and stopped exactly where he had started.

"Good boy, Oonirgluk!" I called out. He stood proudly, head held high.

I rushed up and began patting Oonirgluk. That was a mistake. The rest of the dogs crowded around and entangled me in the lead lines as they ran in circles, jumping for attention. In no time, my ankles were bound together, and the dogs could have easily knocked me down. I shuddered to think what might happen to me if I fell to the ground. Depending on the whim of the dogs, I would either be licked unmercifully or devoured on the spot!

I had read that dogs will often fight if they become too excited or tangled in their traces. These dogs were both excited *and* tangled in their traces—a recipe for trouble.

"Help!" I called to Sally, who was slowly edging away, towards the back of the qamutik. She was still afraid of the dogs when they became excited.

"It's okay, just take Kakpik. He won't bite you," I said. I counted on Kakpik's affection for Sally. Hesitantly, Sally approached the jumping dogs. I unclipped Kakpik and passed him to her.

"Whoa, whoa," I said, trying to calm the others. With Kakpik removed, I was able to free myself from the traces.

We were fortunate that we had learned this important lesson without serious consequences. In the future, I would

Untangling a harness

Our lead dog, Oonirgluk

save my praises and patting until each dog was secured to the long stake-out chain for the night. Once chained out, the dogs were far enough apart that they couldn't reach each other to fight.

With each outing, we learned more about handling the dogs; however, working out our roles with the team caused many arguments between Sally and me during the stressful first weeks. We had read that a team originally trained by a man would respond best to another male voice. With this in mind, we decided that it would be my responsibility to control the dogs.

The problem was, my commands to the dogs were not always obeyed during our first runs.

"Hulla!" Sally shouted to the dogs one morning when she saw that we were on a collision course with a huge block of ice. From behind me on the qamutik, she couldn't help giving directions when she saw that we needed to turn.

"I'm supposed to command the dogs," I snapped. Things weren't going well with the team, and the last thing I needed was Sally's implied criticism.

"Well, they're not listening to you!" she snapped back.

"HULLA! HULLA!" I called harshly to the team. The dogs immediately sensed that I was angry. Subdued, they seemed to lose their enthusiasm for the run. The dogs reflected our mood; their heads hung low and tails drooped. They knew we were having a bad day, and their performance echoed my tone of voice.

Sally and I sat on the qamutik in silence for the rest of the run. I did my best to control the dogs, and Sally refrained from shouting instructions to the team.

This conflict was to plague us for the first weeks of training with the dogs. Sally and I had always shared everything equally—our work and our decision making. Although we knew that only one person could give commands to the dogs, we were completely unprepared for the tensions this would create in our relationship.

"I don't like this one bit," Sally said one day, frustrated almost to tears when the dogs, following my commands, had become entangled on rough ice. "I *told* you to turn right, but you always have your way simply because you give the commands to the dogs."

I didn't like it much either. It seemed that every time the dogs did something wrong, it was my fault. The responsibility was overwhelming. What if my lack of experience got us into a dangerous situation? Would we enjoy the trip or would it be a power struggle with the dogs and each other? Had we taken on more than we could handle?

"I don't want to break up our marriage just because of a dog team," I said after another argument over the matter.

Sally gave me a crooked smile. She was rolling up the dogs' lead lines, readying them for the next trip. "I hardly think we're going to break up over this, Ian," she said. "But it would really help if you'd listen to my directions. How about if you let me do the route finding?"

I agreed to that reluctantly. I had always prided myself on my navigation skills and didn't want to relinquish this task. However, what Sally said made sense, and it would even out our responsibilities.

Sally turned out to be a much better navigator than I would have been because she could devote her full attention to route finding. I found that not having to worry about our route enabled me to keep a closer eye on the dogs. The tension between Sally and me slowly dissolved.

Time and experience also worked a cure. As we grew in confidence over the next weeks, we developed an unshakable faith in each other. Later we would laugh as we recalled these early runs, when anxiety and tension made us bicker.

After our sixth run, Bernard Krako visited and asked how we were doing. I replied that the dogs were pulling well, but they were still not obeying my direction commands.

"I saw you had some trouble getting out of the bay," Bernard said. "Maybe you should have a whip to tell the dogs which way to go."

He explained that I shouldn't use the whip on the dogs but should crack the whip on one side of the team to encourage them to turn towards the other direction.

Bernard went home and returned with a long sealskin whip. We watched him expertly crack the whip again and again. Copying Bernard's overhand motion, I swung my arm as though casting out a fishing line, but using plenty of wrist action.

I managed to score a direct hit on the back of my head as I swung the whip forward. This seemed to entertain Sally and Bernard, so I gave it another try. After flogging myself several times, I finally mastered the six-metre-long whip. The trick was to pause at the end of each forward and reverse swing, and not let the whip play out too quickly.

After my session with Bernard, we bought a sealskin whip from an old hunter. The leather was stiff and dry, so I headed over to Bernard's for some advice.

"You should chew it to make it soft," Bernard suggested.

I looked at the brown stains on the leather, then at Bernard.

"*Atii*, (Go ahead,)" he said, smiling and pointing to the whip.

As soon as I began chewing the whip, my suspicions were confirmed. It tasted like it had been dragged across brown snow behind the dogs.

Bernard laughed when I spat the whip out of my mouth. He was still chuckling when he showed me another way of softening the sealskin—by pulling it back and forth across a chair leg.

Sally and I headed out the next day for another run with the team. Before we started, I practised cracking the whip within sight of the dogs. Every pair of eyes watched, every pair of ears was cocked.

"Maybe they'll listen to my commands now," I said, giving the whip a sharp snap.

The whip did not dampen the dogs' enthusiasm to run. They were as loud and hyperactive as ever. Getting the dogs into position was still quite a feat of strength, though. Oonirgluk and Tokak, the strongest, often pulled me off my feet as they sprinted towards the lead lines.

We had read that we should not discipline the dogs for

enthusiasm during the hookup. This eagerness was a sign of a good dog.

"Good boy, Tokak!" Sally cheered as my kamiks slid out from under me and he dragged me bodily across the snow.

After the usual performance of hooking up the dogs, we headed out of the bay. I soon discovered that using the whip while standing in a stationary spot was very different from cracking it while kneeling on a speeding, swerving qamutik. I let the whip play out behind me, called "Howa-ii," and started to snap the whip forward, aiming for the left side of the team. Instead, the whip caught the last crosspiece of the qamutik then whacked me on the back of my head. My loud yelp had the desired effect though, and the dogs turned the correct way.

"That was great!" Sally said, laughing so hard she almost fell off the qamutik. "You just have to whip yourself every time you want the dogs to turn."

I'm not sure if dogs can laugh, but I had a feeling they were grinning as they resumed their original course. I untangled myself from the whip and tried again. This time, the whip snapped across the back of Sally's head. From then on, she flattened herself on the qamutik every time I raised the whip and lay there, hands over her head, until I was finished.

After several days, I became more adept with the whip. The whip helped Oonirgluk understand which way I wanted him to go. As soon as I snapped the whip and called out a command, he led the team in the correct direction without hesitation.

Oonirgluk not only led the team, but he also behaved differently from the other dogs. He ran with his tail held high and everything about his manner showed that he was the leader of the pack. Oonirgluk often dropped back to water a protruding lump of snow. Then he would shoulder his way between the other dogs to resume his position in the lead.

When we completed each practice run, we patted the dogs and checked them over, looking for any cuts on their feet or other problems. Owning five dogs was like having five children. When Oonirgluk developed a cough, we worried. Was he sick? I checked his nose and eyes for discharge. I listened carefully to his breathing, not really sure what I was trying to detect. Kakpik had a torn ear, the result of a fight during hookup one day. He kept shaking his head and turning it to one side, and I wondered how much pain he was in. Would his wound heal in the cold weather?

Since Tokak rarely bothered to groom his fur, he needed a lot of attention. Most mornings we found a layer of ice coating his fur on the side he had slept on. His feet were often encrusted with ice as well. As more fur stuck to the clumps of ice and snow, his skin became exposed. Usually a run melted all the encrusted ice, but when the temperature dropped to minus forty, the ice didn't melt.

Sally often took care of removing the ice from Tokak's fur. She would slide her bare fingers under the ice and hit the lumps with a stick to break them up. Already we had noticed that Sally could do whatever she wanted with the dogs— including beating their fur with a stick! If I approached any dog with a stick in my hand, he would cower at the far end of his chain.

"That's dedication!" I said when I saw Sally chewing a large lump of ice still attached to Tokak's fur. Sally took another chunk of ice between her teeth and crunched it into small pieces.

"It's the only way I can get the ice off," Sally explained, spitting fur out of her mouth. "But I wish he would wash; his fur reeks of seal fat."

"No one will believe you did this. And to think you used to complain my beard was too furry!" I said.

After our tenth day out, Bernard suggested we join him for a run with his team. We met on the sea ice a kilometre from the village. While we talked, Bernard's eyes passed casually over each dog and our qamutik. Ten centimetres of yellow ice was caked on the front rails.

"Don't let the dogs pee on the qamutik, or by the time you get to Rankin Inlet you'll have a two-foot-high mound of frozen dog piss weighing the sled down!" Bernard said, laughing loudly.

We raced across the ice of Hudson Bay, but Bernard and his team easily outdistanced us. Our Huskies always settled into a steady trot after their first spurt of enthusiasm. An hour later, Bernard stopped and waited for us to catch up.

"Maybe we should change teams for a few minutes," Bernard suggested. It seemed like a strange request, and I felt nervous about running with his dogs. With some hesitation, I changed places.

Within seconds Bernard stopped our team.

"You have Kakpik in the wrong place," he called out. "He should be second, not third."

While Bernard changed the dogs, we took the opportunity to unravel the tangled traces. With the fan-hitch style of hooking up the team, each dog was free to cross from side to side and the traces were easily tangled. I unhooked Kakpik from his lead. Sally held him as I worked with bare fingers to free his line from the spaghetti-like tangle. Bernard watched for a moment before telling us that it would be easier and faster to unhook the lines where they were clipped to the sled.

"Just make sure your lead dog is always clipped in," Bernard cautioned. "If the others get loose, they won't run away without their leader."

Bernard next asked why the rope attached to the front of our sled was four metres long. The tow rope should end just ahead of the qamutik runners, he explained. No wonder we'd had trouble turning! The rope was so long that the sled rarely followed the dogs around corners. When the team turned to avoid an ice block, the qamutik continued to head for the obstacle, often colliding with the ice before being roughly yanked in the new direction.

There was so much to learn. Our journal entries were full of sentences starting with "Bernard says." He had owned a team for several years and was confident and skillful at *qimuksiq* (dogsledding). Best of all, he was willing to share his hard-earned knowledge.

Sally holding dogs during hookup

"The team"

Sally and I went on practice runs with the team almost every day, even in snowstorms, bitterly cold weather, or howling winds—as long as we could see the sun for direction. With each trip, our hookup routine became more efficient, and harnessing the team was no longer such an ordeal. Oonirgluk had grown accustomed to my voice and now understood most of my commands without the aid of the whip. Each trip gave us and the team more confidence. On the good days, Oonirgluk almost pranced along the snow, tail held high.

During January and February the days were short and cold. The temperature rarely climbed above minus thirty-five Celsius. Before each trip we dressed in layer after layer of clothing, starting with Polar-therm underwear and woollen long johns. After three more layers of clothing, we pulled on two pairs of thick duffel socks and caribou-skin kamiks. Finally we donned caribou-skin pants and atigis. By the time we were dressed in all those layers, any differences in body shape were indistinguishable—we both looked like walking blimps.

Some days Sally and I would have preferred to stay inside, but we had to get the dogs into shape for our three-month dogsled journey. Each day we added more weight and travelled farther.

"The dogs are getting stronger, but I'm not," I puffed one afternoon. I was running beside the qamutik up a long hill in order to lighten the load for the dogs.

"Put some pep into it!" Sally urged from her perch on the sled.

"Your turn," I said a few paces later, collapsing onto the qamutik. Not only was I tired, but my hands and feet were numb from the cold after only two hours of travel. What would a full day of sledding be like, I wondered.

We were sledding in conditions that could cause frostbite in seconds—bitterly cold temperatures with a strong wind. Although taking turns running helped us to warm up, we became tired before the circulation returned to our hands and feet. Then it became a mental game: to ignore our cold faces, fingers, and numbed toes; to ignore the overall feeling of cold as it crept to the core of our bodies. As I sat on the sled with the parka ruff pulled tightly around my face, my ice-covered eyelashes began to stick together and my nose lost all sensation.

Sally chills more easily than I do, so I knew that if I was feeling the cold, she must be really suffering. I turned around to see how she was doing. She sat huddled on the sled. Her fur ruff was pulled so closely around her face that I could see only her eyes. I looked into her parka hood and saw that, just above her neoprene face mask, both cheeks had turned whitish grey and waxy.

"Sal, you've got frostbite!" I said.

"I'm all right," she replied. At my insistence, she put her bare fingers to her cheeks. I could see surprise register in her face as she probed the stiff, frostbitten patches.

"I had no idea my cheeks were frozen. I thought I was feeling lumps of ice," she said, "not frostbite." We would have to keep a constant eye on each other and watch for early signs of frostbite.

Between dogsled runs we continued to prepare equipment for the trip. Bernard helped me fashion a push-bar for the qamutik so that I could stand at the rear and control the sled more easily. Sally and I built plywood "grub boxes" and sewed sacks for the dog chains and other equipment. Our new canvas tent finally arrived by air freight, and we spent a day sewing a frost liner and making support poles. Last on our sewing list were windproof cotton covers for our caribou clothing to keep out the icy winds.

After four weeks of day trips, we packed the qamutik with all the equipment we expected to carry on the first leg of our trip. Our gear was piled carefully on the qamutik, wrapped in a sturdy tarp, and lashed down securely.

The team struggled to pull the heavily laden sled. Although they worked with all their hearts, the dogs were unable to swing into their usual trot. And the sled was not yet loaded with the food that we would need for us and the team. After a couple of hours, we turned for home, convinced that we needed at least one more dog.

We found a small Husky named Kimmiq, who we were told was a good worker. At first glance he was a rather unremarkable brown dog, except for his expressive face. He had a way of tilting his head and raising one eyebrow that was endearing. When we introduced him to the team, each dog sniffed him with interest. To our relief, there were no immediate signs of aggression.

As Bernard predicted, Kimmiq ran wide the first time we hooked him up with the team. Actually he tried to run home but was pulled backwards by his harness as the rest of the team surged ahead. After being dragged a couple of times, he must have decided it was easier to cooperate. Still fearful of the other dogs, he ran to one side most of the time, watching the team intently.

Kimmiq seemed to be doing well until his line suddenly caught on a spire of ice that the other dogs had avoided. Before I could slow the qamutik with the snow hook, he was jerked backwards, yelping with surprise and fear.

Kimmiq was smart enough to quickly circle back and run around the obstacle, but he came around the ice spire just as the qamutik slid past. I winced in sympathy as the qamutik rail hit him on the head. Luckily Kimmiq wasn't hurt, although this incident did finally convince him to run with the pack.

With each run, the team became stronger. When we had first started, we could easily run or walk behind the sled on the way home. Now the dogs had the energy to run fast both ways and it was impossible to keep up with them, even with the sled fully loaded. We were surprised at how much difference just one more dog made.

By early March, we had been training for seven weeks. We flew across the hard-packed snow, runners hissing beneath us. The dogs ran with spirit, leaning into their harnesses. Each dog's breath rose into the frigid air like steam from a freight train, and snow crystals flew from their paws. Now and then, a dog would scoop up a mouthful of snow without breaking stride.

For the first time since we had started running the dogs, Sally and I were able to relax. We stretched out on the qamutik, and I shouted encouraging words to the team, "Come on, boys, let's pick it up!" The dogs perked up their ears and surged forward.

I could barely contain my excitement. The dogs were pulling hard, and most importantly, they were pulling in the right direction—our direction.

"I think we're almost ready for the big trip," Sally said, patting me on the back.

"What do you think, boys, are we ready?" I shouted to the team.

Six tails wagged enthusiastically. That was all the confirmation we needed.

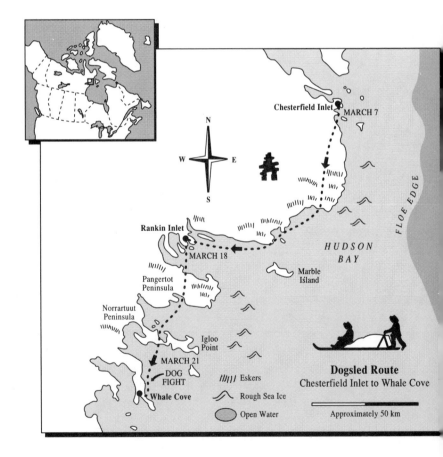

Chesterfield Inlet MARCH 7

N

W E

S

FLOE EDGE

Rankin Inlet
MARCH 18

HUDSON
BAY

Marble
Island

Pangertot
Peninsula

Norrartuut
Peninsula

Igloo
Point

MARCH 21

DOG
FIGHT

Whale Cove

///// Eskers

Rough Sea Ice

Open Water

Dogsled Route
Chesterfield Inlet to Whale Cove

Approximately 50 km

FIFTEEN

Dog Trails

At seven o'clock, long before sunrise on March 7, Sally and I began loading the qamutik for the first leg of our dogsled journey. We heaved two large canvas bags of dog food onto the qamutik and tied down the grub boxes containing our food and cooking equipment. By the time we added our tent, caribou blankets, and other supplies, the tarp barely covered the load. I estimated the qamutik and our load for just eight days weighed 180 kilograms...plus Sally and me.

As Sally and I finished packing, friends dropped by to say goodbye and wish us a successful trip. They watched us harness the dogs, and I wondered if our well-wishers were hoping for the kind of slapstick entertainment that we had provided during our early practice runs.

Sally and I were able to hook up the team quickly and efficiently, but our departure was complicated by the task of uprooting the stake-out chain. During the ten minutes it took me to dig the chain out, Sally held the yapping, eager dogs to prevent them from tangling their traces.

It was quite an act. Sally stood on Oonirgluk's lead line

and held Anukti's harness in her left hand. Two other lead lines were gripped in her right hand. Kakpik, ever restless, was wedged between her knees. Only Arnako was free to roam, but he sat meekly where I had left him.

"Ready?" I asked Sally. This was her cue to release the dogs and jump out of the way.

"Whoop!" I called to the team, and the dogs leaned into their harnesses.

The sled barely moved. Instead of hanging on for the usual blast-off, we had to push to give the sled momentum. Once we had the qamutik moving, the dogs pulled at a steady trot, quite different from their usual energetic sprint. Oonirgluk looked back several times; I'm sure he wondered why the sled was so heavy.

By early afternoon, we were past familiar territory and we both felt a little apprehensive. It was 160 kilometres south along the coast of Hudson Bay to our first resupply point, Rankin Inlet. We hoped to arrive there within eight days. With our limited dogsledding experience, this was a long way to travel on the first leg of our trip, but there was no closer settlement.

From Rankin Inlet, we planned to continue south along the coast to our turnaround point at Arviat. Much of the time we would be travelling on the sea ice close to the shore. The maps showed no roads, no trails, and few landmarks on the thousand-kilometre return trip. To make things more challenging, compass navigation was inaccurate this close to the magnetic pole. We would have to use the position of the sun and the few islands and peninsulas for guidance.

A light snowfall blurred our view, but we continued in a straight line, keeping the faint glow of the sun in front of us. It was eerie out there on the sea ice by ourselves, suspended in a world of white. There were no sounds other than the heavy panting of the dogs and the hiss of the sled runners on the windblown snow.

To avoid a stretch of upheaved, impassable sea ice, we climbed onto the land and followed the coastline. The team pulled well until we came to a lake, which had been swept clear of snow by the howling wind. Because the rocky lakeshore had also been blown clear of snow, we had no choice but to cross the lake.

The dogs veered away from the lake, wary of the smooth, slippery ice. I stopped the team and herded them onto the lake, but Kimmiq and Arnako whined and locked their front legs, refusing to step onto the ice.

"Come on, boys!" Sally called, urging the team towards her. To encourage them along, she walked—or rather, shuffled—ahead of the dogs, barely managing to stay on her feet..Slipping and sliding, I pushed the sled. Even the dogs, with their claws and four legs, had to scrabble for purchase on the slippery surface.

Kimmiq wouldn't do his share of the work as we crossed the ice. First he tried to return to the shore. Then he refused to pull, and his sprawling form was dragged along. When the team reached the opposite shore, a snarling Oonirgluk turned back and headed for the delinquent dog, ears forward, hackles raised, and tail up. Kimmiq cowered, then rushed to take his proper position with the other dogs. There was no doubt that Oonrigluk was the boss.

Once past the slippery ice, the dogs pulled steadily up a steep hill bordering the lake. Sally and I took turns walking until the route levelled out. We stopped around three-thirty when the dogs began to tire. Sally and I also needed enough time to set up camp before the sun dropped below the horizon at five o'clock.

Six weary dogs flopped onto the snow while we unpacked the long chain and anchored it in place with aluminum stakes. We clipped each dog onto the chain then immediately removed their harnesses so that the chewers would not have time to devour the webbing. Once unharnessed, the dogs curled into balls with tails wrapped around noses.

I was so tired from our first day of travel that I was tempted to flop down on the snow beside the dogs. But there was no time for rest yet; we still had to set up camp and feed the team. Although we could cut snow blocks, they were too granular for igloo building. Instead, we set up our canvas tent and placed a row of snow blocks around the perimeter for protection from the wind.

With buckets and axe in hand, Sally and I headed to a nearby pond just off the sea ice. By melting ice instead of snow, we would save fuel and time—a pot of ice yielded almost a full pot of water, but a pot of dry snow produced only a few mugs of liquid. We would need a full bucket of water just for the dog food.

"Taste it and see if it's salty," Sally suggested.

I lifted a piece to my mouth. My lips and tongue immediately stuck to the ice!

"Outh, thith ithe ith thtuck," I mumbled as Sally burst out laughing. At least I remembered not to tear the ice off my tongue. The more I complained, the more Sally laughed until she was rolling in the snow. I failed to see the humour in my predicament, but finally the warmed ice parted from my tongue.

"Well, was it salty or not?" Sally asked.

It wasn't. We chipped at the ice with the axe, then carried two full buckets of ice back to the tent. By the time we had melted the ice, mixed the dog food, and fed the dogs, it was five-thirty and almost dark.

We were up with the sun at eight the next morning. The dogs ignored us as we packed up camp, even sleeping through the din of Sally beating the frost out of the tent liner. They started to show some interest as we opened the tarp on the qamutik.

Loading the qamutik was a slow process because we hadn't yet worked out a system of packing efficiently. This time we were careful to put the items we needed for the day on top. Yesterday we'd done without extra mitts because they were buried somewhere in the pile of gear. When everything was packed, I lashed the load down with one long rope, weaving it back and forth over the qamutik.

Six snoozing dogs suddenly came to life when Sally pulled out the harnesses. Even though our first day had been hard work for the dogs, they were as enthusiastic as ever. The hookup went smoothly, and we headed across the land.

By midday, the dogs needed a rest. So did Sally and I; the snow was so deep that we'd taken turns pushing the qamutik for much of the way. While Sally and I munched on frozen salami and rock-hard chunks of cheese, the dogs ate snow. The dogs enjoyed the break and rolled onto their backs to rub where the harnesses compressed their fur.

Kimmiq never rested for longer than a minute. He weaved in and out of the lines, dug into the snow, and pounced on imaginary prey. The rest of the dogs sprawled across the snow. Oonirgluk lay facing us, broad head resting on his front paws. His tongue hung out the side of his mouth and moulded around his long, sharp incisors. As he panted, steam rose into the icy air. Each dog was wreathed in hoar-frost, and saliva had frozen into icy beards under their chins.

Sally and I poured tea from a thermos to wash down our frozen lunch, but after only a few minutes the dogs were up and eager to go.

"We'd better head out before they get all tangled up again," I said. I gulped my tea and threw my cup into the grub box.

"I sure wish the dogs would take a longer rest," Sally replied, securing the grub box as the dogs leapt against their lines.

After two more hours of travel, the dogs began to slow noticeably. We called it a day. Sally and I began a routine that would continue through the trip. Once the dogs were staked out, we set up the tent together. As I built a snow-wall for protection from the wind, Sally dragged our camping gear and grub boxes into the tent. There was no floor in this tent, so our caribou furs went directly on the snow. On top of these, Sally placed our zipped-together synthetic sleeping bags and spread a caribou-skin blanket on top. We hoped this combination of old and new would keep us warm, even on the coldest nights.

I had started the second row of snow blocks when I heard Sally pumping the stove. From inside the tent came the dull hiss of the small Coleman, the clang of a pot lid, and the scrape of Sally's ulu cutting pieces of snow to melt for water. As soon as the snow wall was finished, I headed inside for a quick cup of tea before feeding the dogs. Mamaaq had taught us this habit of having that precious mug of warmth before dealing with a cold task.

When it came time to feed the team, Sally held each dog out of the way while I ladled out a ration of Purina Dog Chow. Sally's job wasn't easy—it was almost impossible for her to hold them, especially when wearing her slippery caribou-skin kamiks.

Kimmiq, as always, was the most difficult. As Sally held his chain, he leapt, squirmed, twisted, and turned in all directions. Sally was knocked off her feet and trampled by Kimmiq, who was like a hyperactive kangaroo.

"Help!" Sally yelled as she lay on the ground, still trying to hold Kimmiq as he did the polka on her stomach.

Grabbing Kimmiq's collar, I lifted him until his front feet were off the ground. Kimmiq wriggled and danced, bashing me painfully in the jaw with his head.

"Now you know what I go through at feeding time," Sally said, grinning as I nursed my bruised jaw.

Like fur-clad vacuum cleaners, the dogs devoured their servings of food. Then they seemed to look at us accusingly, as if to say, "So, what's for supper?" We knew five cups of kibbles plus lard or seal fat for each dog met all their energy and nutrition requirements, but I suppose gulping down the soft food in seconds left them feeling unsatisfied.

Sally and I returned to the tent and collapsed on the caribou hides, exhausted. I was surprised how warm the tent seemed (relatively speaking) when the small stove was heating a pot of water. When it was minus thirty outside, minus fifteen inside the tent was luxuriously warm.

After supper, we removed our caribou clothes and used them for pillows and extra insulation from the snow. By the time we tucked our damp duffel socks, wool socks, and mitt liners into the sleeping bag to dry, there seemed barely enough room for us to squeeze in.

By morning, an intricate pattern of ice crystals had

formed on the rim of the caribou blanket. I changed position and a shower of frost landed on my cheek, first cold, then wet as each crystal melted. Not interested in studying the crystals, I tucked my head under the blanket and hoped Sally would light the stove.

I lay hidden under the caribou blanket until I heard Sally shut off the stove. Tea was ready. Ah, tea! It's the drink of the north. Like magic, a warm glow spread through me when I sipped the hot liquid. As I tipped my mug to drain the last of the tea, I noticed a rim of ice crystals already encircling the mug. Not feeling so warm any more, I pulled on my atigi, but remained under the caribou blanket. We lingered over breakfast and a second cup of hot liquid before dressing for another day on the trail.

When I stepped outside the tent, my nose hairs froze almost instantly. Ice crystals floated in the morning air, and the weak sun offered little warmth. I pulled my hood tightly around my face. Checking the thermometer, I found the thin red line hovering at minus forty Celsius—the bottom of the scale. Sally and I packed up, moving quickly to keep warm. Within an hour, the qamutik was loaded and we set out across the tundra.

All morning, a steady wind ruffled the fur on the backs of our caribou qulittaqs. My cheeks became numb. Removing a mitt, I held my hand against my face, warming one cheek then the other. From then on, I made a point of checking Sally's face every few minutes as well. I knew that her cheeks would easily become frostbitten where the skin was tender from previous freezings.

"Thanks, partner," Sally said, smiling as I warmed her face with my bare hand.

Throughout the day, the wind increased, bringing the windchill temperature lower and lower. By the time we stopped, we decided it wasn't a night to spend in our tent. Sally began cutting snow blocks while I outlined the shape of the igloo with my snow knife.

An hour and a half later, I reached up from inside and lowered the final block into place. With the igloo completed,

Feeding time!

Building an igloo after a day of sledding

the moan of the wind was silenced. All was quiet, except for the dull thumping of Sally packing snow into the cracks outside. I cut an entrance hole with the snow knife, and Sally passed in the sleeping skins, bags, and grub boxes.

I lit the stove and cut a fist-size ventilation hole in the dome. While our soup simmered on the stove, the igloo slowly warmed with rolling clouds of steam.

"I thought I'd never feel warm again," Sally said as she pulled off her mitts and pushed back her parka hood. She had been out in the wind much longer than I had, and her eyebrows were thick with frost.

In the half-light of dusk, I took one last trip outside to check on the dogs. The igloo glowed blue-green as lantern light radiated through the blocks of snow, outlining the dome against the dark sky. Each translucent block was outlined by white light. I could see Sally's shadow move across the dome as she passed in front of the lantern.

The next morning, we emerged to a changed landscape. Soft snow had drifted against the igloo and qamutik, and each dog was outlined by a crescent of snow on its leeward side. I stepped onto a drift, and unexpectedly sank down to my knees. The wind had been strong enough to shift the new snow about but not fierce enough to pack it into the usual concrete-like drifts.

We sledded back down to the sea ice, hoping for a fast run on the frozen surface. It was not any easier; the ice was covered with soft snow, and the dogs sank up to their stomachs in the drifts. The dogs closed the fan hitch and bunched together to walk in Oonrigluk's trail. They strained hard. Even six Huskies were not enough to haul us and the load through the soft snow.

It was so difficult for the dogs that Sally and I both had to get off the qamutik to lighten the load. We took turns pushing the sled through the snow. At the deepest snow-drifts, it took our combined strength to keep the qamutik moving. When the dogs turned to avoid ice blocks, we had to wrestle the heavy qamutik into the new direction.

It was back-breaking, lung-freezing, muscle-pulling

work. Our hopes of travelling twenty kilometres a day were sinking in the deep snow of early March.

After six more days of pushing the sled through soft snow, we reached Rankin Inlet, where we rested and picked up supplies. On March 18, with their stomachs full of fresh meat, the dogs were eager to go again.

"I don't know what makes them want to pull," I said, admiring the enthusiasm of the dogs. I was still tired and did not feel as energetic or as enthusiastic as the dogs.

We continued south along the coastline, struggling through the deep snow that covered the sea ice. I wished for winds to blast the snow into the usual hard-packed surface, even though I knew such a wind would bring bitter cold. As each day passed, we became more trail-weary. Each time we felt like giving up, Sally and I took inspiration from the dogs, who kept pulling despite our depressing progress. Our momentum slowed even more when we came to high ridges of ice blocking our way. These pressure ridges were caused by the sea ice settling on reefs when the tide dropped.

"You scout ahead and find a route," I suggested to Sally when we reached a formidable ridge of ice blocks. "I'll hold the dogs until you come back." That was easier said than done. As soon as Sally walked ahead, the dogs tried to follow. I repeated "Whoa!" over and over again as the dogs tugged at their harnesses.

Sally's small form disappeared among the towering blocks of ice. I could almost feel the awesome power of the sea currents that had created the massive jumble of ice blocks and pressure ridges. It was as if a wave-torn sea had frozen instantly.

When Sally returned, the dogs followed her footprints through the maze of ice. As the qamutik crashed over each block of ice, the traces often became snagged, jerking the dogs off balance. It took us two hours to work our way through one kilometre of bad ice. Finally the qamutik rose over the last ridge. Then it hurtled down the near-vertical slope on the other side.

"I'm glad that's . . ." My words were cut short as the sled

Ian catching his breath

Tired dogs

dove straight down into the snow and came to a jolting stop. I somersaulted over the push-bar, and the dogs yelped with surprise as they were jerked off their feet. Sally lay beside the qamutik, sprawled in the snow.

One runner was buried in the snow. Groaning with effort, we tried to move the qamutik backwards.

"Pull," I grunted as I heaved on the tow rope. The qamutik wouldn't budge. As I dug down with the shovel I came to the sickening conclusion that the runner was broken. The runner had been driven deep into a crack in the ice.

"We'll have to chop it out," I said, reaching for the axe. After five minutes of chopping the ice, I saw that the runner was bent inward at a sharp angle. Another five minutes of chopping freed the runner. As we lifted the qamutik, the runner sprang back into place with only a hairline crack to indicate the stress it had been subjected to. Sally and I breathed sighs of relief—it would have been almost impossible to repair a broken runner. Without a qamutik, we would have a long walk to Whale Cove.

We had just started off again when Arnako stumbled and let out a series of anguished yelps. He had a line wrapped around a rear leg.

Before I could heave the snow hook off the sled, Tokak jumped Arnako. Huskies love a good fight and will attack any member of the pack showing weakness. Anukti and the others joined in a fur-flying, growling, snarling, yelping, bloody, all-out dog fight. I ran forward and pulled dogs off the pile, but they jumped back in faster than I could pull them off, tangling themselves—and me—in the lead lines.

Frightening red blotches of blood soaked into the snow. Arnako squealed pitifully. As his yelps of pain increased, I became frantic. We hadn't been prepared for a fight like this and had never discussed what to do.

"They're going to kill him! Grab Tokak!" Sally screamed, pulling on the nearest lead line.

"What do you think I'm trying to do?" I hollered. But the dogs were so involved in the free-for-all that I couldn't grab any of them.

The noise was terrifying as the snarling dogs tore chunks of fur from Arnako. Both Sally and I shouted at the dogs, commanding them to do this or do that. The dogs didn't hear us.

Finally I had no choice but to rain blows upon the dogs from my fists and feet. Even these they ignored. As I stepped between fighting dogs, my knee received a painful bite that had been intended for another dog. Now I was afraid not only for Arnako but also for myself. If a lead line wrapped around my ankle and I fell, they'd attack me, too.

"Do something!" I yelled.

"Like what?" Sally yelled back, terror in her voice. She didn't wait for an answer but threw off her mitts. Grabbing Oonrigluk's line, she hauled him away and tied him to the qamutik.

The dogs were becoming increasingly upset. So were Sally and I. We shouted instructions to each other, and that only made the dogs wilder. The fight was out of control.

Eventually, though, I was somehow able to haul Tokak from the fray. Sally took him and tied him away from the others. As soon as Tokak was removed, the fight was over.

My heart was beating as hard as I had been beating on the dogs. My arms and legs were shaking, and my left knee was throbbing from the dog bite. I could feel the dampness where blood soaked through my pants as I limped over to the qamutik, dragging Anukti with me so I could tie him up.

"I think we need to work on our dog-fight management skills," I joked weakly to Sally. She looked at me tight-lipped and silent as she worked with bare hands to untangle a mass of ropes wrapped around Arnako.

I checked the rest of the dogs, and when I next looked at Sally, she was crouched by the sled, rocking back and forth. Her hands were tucked under her armpits and tears streamed down her face. I wasn't sure if her tears were from the pain of frostbite or shock of the dog fight.

I placed Sally's hands under my parka where they could warm against my bare skin.

"Are you okay?" I asked.

"I think so . . . but poor Arnako," Sally said, as I dried her tears. Arnako looked terrible. His front legs, nose, and both ears were bleeding, and he had a deep puncture wound in his neck. Scarlet blood was mixed with gobs of saliva in his matted white fur. He yelped each time we tried to move him. It didn't surprise me that Arnako was the one to be attacked—he was the weakest of the dogs.

After an hour of coaxing, Arnako finally rose to his feet. He was a dejected-looking creature. His tail was tucked between his legs and his head hung low. I tied him to the back of the sled, and much to our surprise, he ran when I gave the command to go. He was still traumatized though. Every time the sled thumped down, he yelped. When we stopped for a rest, he cowered in the snow, whimpering.

Tokak had been the worst scrapper and we would have to watch him closely. After the dog fight, I was much firmer with the dogs, but Sally and I were both nervous each time we stopped. As usual, the dogs didn't rest for long. They wandered as far as their lead lines permitted. I kept a constant eye on the dogs, ready to intervene at any moment.

"Looks like we still have seven or eight kilometres to Whale Cove," I said, checking the map.

"I don't want to camp out here with Arnako in such a mess," Sally said. "Let's keep going."

The dogs were still pulling hard and the snow conditions had improved, so I agreed to go for it. If all went well, we could get to Whale Cove in two hours.

As we neared town in the low light of late afternoon, wisps of windblown snow snaked across the surface of the ice. I turned my head away from the cold wind. When I next looked up, another dog team had materialized out of the blowing snow and was heading across the ice towards us. An older Inuit man dressed from head to toe in caribou clothing stopped his team near us.

"*Nani nunaqaqpit?* (What place did you come from?)" the man asked as he walked towards us.

"*Igluliarjuk,*" I replied, using the Inuktitut name for Chesterfield Inlet.

He clapped his mittened hands together and said something in Inuktitut, which I couldn't quite understand. Nodding his head, he looked at our team, his eyes resting for a moment on Arnako, tied to the back of the qamutik. Then he looked at me, and there was a flash of understanding in the meeting of our eyes. He must have sensed what we had been through.

He embraced me with a huge, caribou-clad bear hug. His actions told me that he was thrilled we had travelled so far by dog team. We were, after all, probably the first Qablunaaqs he'd ever met travelling by dog team. I felt a lump rise in my throat at this warm welcome to Whale Cove.

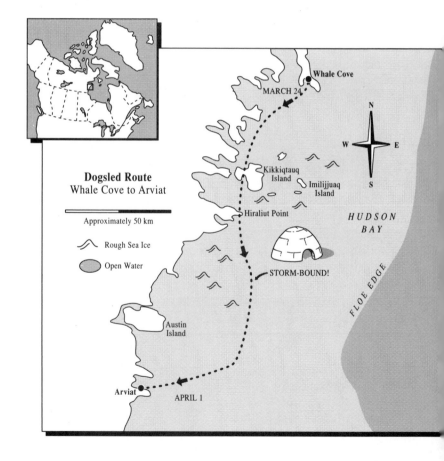

Dogsled Route
Whale Cove to Arviat

Approximately 50 km

Rough Sea Ice

Open Water

Whale Cove

MARCH 24

Kikkiqtauq
Island

Imilijjuaq
Island

Hiraliut Point

HUDSON
BAY

STORM-BOUND!

FLOE EDGE

Austin
Island

Arviat

APRIL 1

N
W · E
S

SIXTEEN

Pulling Hard

"I feel like we pushed this thing all the way from Chesterfield Inlet," I said, as we sledded into Whale Cove.

"That's because we did!" was Sally's weary reply. It had taken us two weeks to travel only 250 kilometres down the coast. Sally and I looked forward to a chance to rest in this small hamlet; we hoped to stay with Mamaaq Innakatsik's daughter Leah.

I held the team while Sally ran into the first house to ask where Leah lived.

"She's at the pink and blue house down the road," was the answer, and off we went at full speed. Turning the corner as directed, we were dismayed to see that *twelve* of the hamlet's forty houses were pink and blue. After another enquiry, we pulled up to the fourth house.

Sally disappeared into the house while I held the dogs. A few minutes later, to my great surprise, Mamaaq came out, beaming her wonderful smile! Mamaaq gave me such long hug I thought she would never let go. Then she took a step back and extended a hand, and we exchanged a more formal once-up-and-down handshake, still grinning broadly. I felt so happy that Mamaaq, who had taught us so much, had a chance to see us with our dog team.

As soon as we entered the house after chaining out the dogs, Mamaaq handed us each a piece of bannock and a bowl of cooked caribou meat. The pleased expressions on our faces and the quickly emptied bowls showed our appreciation for this Inuit tradition of feeding travellers as soon as they arrive.

After we had eaten, Leah translated our adventures for Mamaaq. A while later, Sally asked how we should care for our kamiks, because our feet were often cold. Mamaaq looked horrified when she put her hand inside Sally's kamiks and felt a thick layer of ice. After a mild scolding, she showed us how to turn the kamiks inside out so that we could easily beat the frost from the kamiks before it accumulates and turns to ice. Mamaaq also suggested drying the kamiks over the warm lantern and hanging them from the top of the tent at night.

One piece of equipment that urgently needed attention during this stopover was our tent. The door was held closed by only three ties, and on most nights snow had blown into the tent. Leah gave us a zipper from an old sleeping bag, and I began sewing it onto the flap of the tent. Leah offered to help after watching me for a few minutes.

"I'm a good sewer because I was born in the summer," Leah said as she deftly stitched the canvas. She explained that Mamaaq had put spiders between her fingers when she was a baby to ensure her fingers would be nimble and fast, like a spider spinning a web.

Our visit was like old times: communicating with laughter, smiles, and short Inuktitut phrases. Matthew "helped" Sally and Mamaaq sew new soles on our kamiks, and they seemed to be continually looking for the ulu or thread or needles. Our time was spent visiting neighbours and drinking endless cups of tea. In between visits, we were kept busy making other adjustments to our equipment and preparing for the next leg of our trip.

Sally and I picked up the shipment of supplies that our

expediter had sent from Yellowknife. When a neighbour saw us lugging large bags of dog food to the house, he generously offered us Arctic char for the dogs. Although the fish was heavier than our dried dog food, it would be easier to toss chunks of frozen char to the dogs on a stormy night than prepare the dry food.

As a special treat that night, we fed each dog half an Arctic char. I tossed a three-kilogram chunk to Anukti, who leapt into the air, catching it neatly in his teeth.

"Hope they appreciate this," I said to Sally. "Each piece would cost twenty bucks in a southern fish market."

I looked over the dogs as they devoured their supper. With great gusto, they tore into their portion and consumed the entire fish, bones and all, within minutes. I had been told that if a dog wasn't feeling well, it wouldn't eat. These dogs were obviously healthy. Even Arnako was recovering his appetite, and we hoped that penicillin tablets hidden in his supper would ward off any infections.

Our only problem was that we needed another dog to pull the heavy load. Sally and I weren't keen about pushing the sled all the way to Arviat and back! Leah told us of a man named Teenar who might sell us a dog. Teenar was quiet and reserved when we first met him, but he warmed up when he learned we were Mamaaq's tiguaq.

"Unakuluk!" he laughed, calling me by the nickname Mamaaq had given me. She had told him all about the pranks I used to play on her. Sally and I were delighted when he let us choose any dog we wanted from his team. We studied his dogs as he told us about each one.

Sally and I quickly agreed that all the dogs met our exacting standards—their tails wagged furiously when they saw us and they didn't bite. The biggest dog seemed to be our best choice. We were never sure if we were saying the name properly, but we called the new dog Tuaa. We introduced him to the other dogs and chained him with his teammates.

After the dog fight, tangles, and other problems of our first two weeks of travel, Sally and I had many questions to ask

Teenar. We realized that we still had much to learn about dogsledding. Teenar readily shared his knowledge, from how to plane the qamutik runners so they would slide more easily, to suggestions on how to control the dogs better. His most important tip was that we should make them lie down at each rest stop until we were ready to go—that way we would avoid snarled lines and snarling dogs.

"It sure would be nice to drink a whole mug of tea before the dogs jump up," I confided to Teenar. Making the dogs lie down will be like trying to make seven energetic kids sit still, I thought to myself. Now I realized that we had allowed the dogs to develop their bad habits; we had never made them lie down at rest stops. It would take some time to change their behaviour.

We asked Teenar for his suggestions on a route to Arviat, more than two hundred kilometres away. Sally spread our maps out across the floor, and Teenar drew a pencil line down the coast. The meandering line crossed the land in one place and swung far out onto Hudson Bay at another to avoid rough sea ice.

It seemed a lifetime ago that we had looked over these maps in the outfitter's shop in Vancouver. My mind flashed back to the new boots and shiny pots that had held the maps down then. Now a caribou bone held down one side and an ulu rested on a corner. We were learning the Inuktitut names for the landmarks and looking over the same maps from a totally different perspective.

The next morning we decided to go on a short run with Tuaa to see how well he worked with the other dogs.

"*Qimuksiq oubloumi?* (Would you like to go dogsledding today?)" I asked Mamaaq. I thought a short trial run with our new dog would be a good idea.

"Ii, matna!" she replied, her eyes lighting up.

Dressed in Sally's qulittaq that she had helped sew, Mamaaq stood back and watched us hook up the dogs. I glanced over to Mamaaq and was secretly pleased to see her smiling and nodding her approval.

"Oonirgluk! Whoop!" and we were off.

"Hulla, hulla," I called, and we went sliding around a sharp turn towards the sea ice. Unencumbered by the usual heavy load, the dogs enjoyed running flat out. The qamutik rattled over a series of bumps, and I looked back to see if Mamaaq was all right. I should have known better; she had spent countless days on qamutiks and looked as comfortable as if she was on an easy chair.

As we headed out of the bay, I named each dog in turn. Mamaaq laughed at Anukti, eater of turds. Squinting into the sun, she watched the dogs and made a comment now and then. Her laughter continued as she pointed to the back end of Arnako, which wiggled as he ran.

Sally and I were pleased with how well the run went. The dogs behaved well, and even Tuaa quickly found his place in the pack. He ran well, not pulling hard yet, but a definite asset to the team. Best of all, the dogs listened to my every command and ran without even growling at their teammates.

We spent another day in Whale Cove before continuing our journey down the coast. On March 24, with one last, long hug, we said our farewell to Mamaaq. As the team pulled us away, I turned and waved to her. In many ways, Mamaaq was travelling with us—her caribou clothing would keep us warm, the lessons she had taught us would keep us safe, and the memory of her smile would keep us going.

As we headed onto the sea ice, we sailed over a ridge of upheaved shore ice and landed with a tooth-rattling crash. The qamutik tipped precariously to one side. I talked to Sally, never taking my eyes off the dogs.

"Which side of the island should we go?" I asked. The map hung in a pouch below the push-bar, where Sally usually stood. Hearing no reply, I turned around to see why Sally wasn't answering. I was surprised to see her in the distance—chasing us across the ice. By the time she reached the sled, Sally was red-faced and had steam rising from her neck and cuffs.

"Caribou clothes aren't designed for jogging," Sally said,

puffing as she cooled down on the qamutik.

Up came our snow hooks and we were off again, from zero to ten kilometres an hour in seconds, the dogs' feet a blur of motion. They kept up this speed for almost ten minutes, then slowed to a more sensible trot. With our team now seven dogs strong, Sally and I were able to ride most of the time. We had to run alongside the qamutik only where the snow drifts were deep or the route went uphill.

Even Arnako was pulling hard, back in his usual position in the team. His wounds were healing slowly though, and it would still be a few days before he recovered what little spunk he'd had before the fight. Sally and I would have to watch him closely to make sure the other dogs didn't harass him.

With Teenar's advice in mind, I became stricter with the team. Feeling like a tyrant, I cracked the whip over the dogs' heads at each rest stop. Finally they understood that I expected them to lie down each time we halted.

At one of these stops, the dogs became restless after a few minutes. I was unable to make them lie down again, and Kimmiq dashed from side to side, snapping at Tokak, who was closest to him. Before I could intervene, Tokak turned with a growl and lunged towards Kimmiq.

"Stop him!" Sally shrieked. All the dogs noticed the distress in her voice and turned to see what was happening.

"Tokak!" I called angrily, cracking the whip over his head. He lay down in the snow, a low growl rumbling in his throat.

I turned to Sally and saw tears trickling down her cheeks. "What's the matter? They didn't fight."

"I can't help it. Every time a dog growls I remember them trying to rip Arnako apart."

Tokak's growl became louder, and he slowly rose to his feet.

"No more Mister Nice Guy," I said gruffly. Dragging Tokak by his harness, I separated him from the team. Then I swatted him across the nose with a mitt. This big, tough Husky was really a coward in disguise, and he yelped as if I had beaten him mercilessly. Tokak returned to the team with his tail between his legs.

"Every dog was watching," Sally said when I returned.

"I'll show them who's boss. The next offender gets two mitts across the nose!" Tokak's howls must have been convincing. Even Kimmiq lay quietly in the snow.

Untangling the lead lines was still a difficult procedure, and I used a stern voice to keep the dogs lying down. After unhooking all the lead lines except Oonirgluk's, I held the bundle of lines while Sally sorted out the twisted mess. This task could not be accomplished with bulky mitts, so Sally worked quickly, wearing only thin gloves. I saw her lips draw tight as the cold penetrated her fingers. After being frostbitten during the dog fight, Sally's fingers had blistered and the ends were now cracked and peeling. They were very sensitive to the cold. Although Sally never said anything, I often noticed her sitting with her hands tucked in her armpits to keep them warm.

That evening we camped among towering blocks of ice on the sea ice. Mamaaq had told us that it was warmer on the sea ice than on the land. It made sense; the water underneath the ice was warmer than the frozen land.

We devoured a gooey pot of macaroni and cheese, then wrote our journal entries by the light of our Coleman lantern. The ink in our pens had frozen long ago, and even pencils barely marked the paper. When my fingers became too numb to write, I began the nightly routine of drying mitts, gloves, socks, and duffels over the hot lantern.

"Glove alert!" Sally called as the unpleasant smell of burning caribou hair wafted through the tent. The gloves and other clothing being dried required constant tending. A hole in a mitt or sock would be a catastrophe.

Over steaming cups of tea we talked about the day, pleased that our new dog, Tuaa, was fitting in so well with the team. Sally and I sat with a caribou blanket wrapped around our shoulders as we compared our impressions of the pleasures and problems of the day. While travelling, we were too busy with the dogs to chat.

"Nice to relax after a long day," I said, sipping my tea.

Moments later a loud *boom!* made me almost jump out of my kamiks. A three-finger-wide crack appeared in the ice—right between my legs. The crack continued from one side of the the tent to the other. I stared down, expecting the fissure to widen at any moment.

"Do you think we should move the tent?" I asked.

Before Sally could answer, we heard the thunder of ice cracking nearby. After listening to the rumbling for a few minutes, we decided to stay put. Our camp was in as good a location as any, and trying to find a better site in the dark would be pointless.

All night long, we felt the ice trembling and shifting beneath us. Fortunately no other cracks ran through the tent—we'd had enough excitement for one evening!

At dawn we surveyed the many cracks in the ice. Several parallel cracks ran near our camp, but none were wider than a few centimetres. Each time the tide went out, the ice settled on the uneven shore, buckling with ear-splitting noises. Cracks were just a part of life when camping on the sea ice, though I never did get used to the feel of the ice trembling under me at night.

Not long after we began travelling again, we encountered an overwhelming mass of broken ice. Gargoyles, obelisks, pyramids, and other odd-shaped ice sculptures lurked in the piles of ice. There was no chance of finding our way through the maze of upheaved, twisted ice, four times our height.

"Howa-ii," I called, turning the dogs towards land. Our land route avoided the jumble of sea ice, but travel was slower in the soft, snow-filled hollows and over the rocky, wind-swept eskers. Late that afternoon, we stopped for a rest where we were sheltered from the wind. The dogs were tired and immediately lay down while Sally rummaged in the grub box for a snack. Because we were always hungry, we nibbled throughout the day. The only way to satisfy our craving for fats and sugars was with hourly snacks of nuts, candies, dried fruit, and chocolate-covered peanuts. We also devoured great quantities of chocolate and fruit cake.

Pulling Hard

Just as Sally was passing me my ration of chocolate, two Arctic hares bounded in front of the dogs, only ten metres away. In an instant, all the dogs sprang to their feet, howling and leaping against their lines in an effort to chase the hares.

Thinking fast, Sally jumped onto the rear snow hook while I pulled on the tow rope to the dogs. My effort was ineffective; one dog alone could easily drag me across the tundra. I abandoned that tactic and grabbed the whip instead.

"Whoa, whoa," I ordered, standing between the hares and the dogs while I brandished the whip. I wondered if the team might run me over at any moment.

One hare hopped away, zigzagging across the snow. But the other hare hopped only a short distance. Then the animal stopped—white on white as it blended with the landscape. The problem was, the dogs knew it was still there.

The dogs eventually calmed down, although they continued to study the hare. Each dog sat at attention, ears perked forward and nose twitching. I breathed a sigh of relief when the hare finally bounded across the snow and out of sight.

That evening, we patted every dog, regardless of their behaviour during the day. This daily ritual of stomach scratching and ear rubbing was therapeutic for us as well as the dogs. I was always amazed how just one sloppy, wet lick could take me away from the problems of the day and raise my spirits. I found it was very soothing to have the dogs' unconditional affection, and they loved the attention.

Sally and I each had a favourite dog to whom we could whisper any confidence, who would just listen and not judge or comment as we talked. My favourite was Oonirgluk, and I praised him endlessly for his leadership. Sally talked at length to Kakpik while she rubbed his ears and warmed her fingers in his thick fur. Whenever she tried to walk away, he would playfully tug at the sash hanging from her atigi.

The only dog we didn't like very much was Kimmiq. He

had an irritating habit of constantly crossing back and forth over the traces when the team was running. I snarled at him each time we had to untangle the lead lines. He had no canine friends either. As soon as he was safely chained out of reach of any other dogs, he would growl at his neighbours.

"Quiet, Kimmiq!" I shouted from the tent one evening when I heard his low rumble.

A while later, we heard the wolflike howl of Oonirgluk echo in the still night air. The wavering sound became louder and more intense as other dogs joined in, creating a harmony of howls.

Ow, ow, owhoo-oo-oo. Through the thin walls of the tent, I could hear each dog clearly as the notes swelled and faded. Oonrigluk, Anukti, and Arnako were all baritones, blending together in their dog-song. Kakpik and Kimmiq had high voices, the sopranos of the septet. Tokak was out of tune, much in character with his laid-back manner. Tuaa didn't always join in, but when he did, his voice was distinctly the tenor, weaving in and out in perfect harmony.

We drifted to sleep as the howling of our seven travel companions faded into the cold night air. It was the perfect dog-teamer's lullaby.

Camping on the Barren Lands

Caribou crossing the Thelon River

Canoeing through the Thelon Canyon

A lone muskox watching us drift by

Mamaaq

Winter sunset

Ice fishing in November

179

Oonirgluk and Sally

Sally at the push-bar

Evening in an igloo

Our dogs pulling hard

The team taking a rest

Our igloo illuminated by a lante

Tokak and Sally

A snow knife

Taking a rest by an igloo

Canoeing on Hudson Bay

Arctic char

Canoeing among icebergs

S E V E N T E E N

Storm-bound

As we continued south along the rough sea ice, blue sky gradually gave way to herringbone clouds and swirling snow. By noon, we were in the midst of a fierce winter storm. The tracks of the qamutik and the footprints of the dogs were erased as quickly as they were made.

"We'd better find a place to dig in," Sally called to me, shouting over the howling wind.

I looked at the dogs, who were running with their tails low, ears flat, and eyes almost closed against the stinging, wind-driven snow.

"Okay," I called back. "As soon as we find snow for an igloo. The tent will never stay up in this!"

The wind increased until the blowing snow obscured objects below our waists. We knew the dogs were there, somewhere, but only because the sled was moving steadily forward.

I turned the team towards land, hoping for good snow at the edge of the sea ice. The wind sucked the warmth from our bodies and we became chilled to the bone. The wind was gusting to more than forty kilometres per hour, giving a windchill factor of a numbing minus sixty Celsius. We had never experienced such low temperatures. It was so cold that frost collected on everything—our parkas, the dogs, the qamutik. I looked at Sally and saw her turning white around the edges: her eyebrows, cheeks, and the ruff of her hood were frosted with ice. I worried about her frostbitten cheeks.

My beard turned into a white mask of ice. When my frost-covered eyelashes stuck together, sealing my lids closed, I muttered a low curse that steamed into the frigid air. Each time my eyelashes stuck together, I had to pull off a mitt and melt the frost between bare fingers. My hands were slow with cold, so I banged them together to restore circulation.

It was too cold to continue. The dogs had slowed to a walk, heads turned away from the wind.

"This will have to do," I said to Sally as I tested a drift with my snow knife. "Do you think you could stake out the dogs on your own?"

"If you keep an eye on them—they never listen to me!" Sally replied.

I nodded to Sally, but as soon as I stepped a few paces away, the dogs and Sally disappeared into the swirling snow. At least the dogs were upwind, I thought; even though I couldn't see them, I could hear if any problems developed.

Snow knife in hand, I set to work building an igloo. As I started the first row, I thought back to the many days I had spent practising the art of igloo building. Those days of struggling with falling snow blocks and obtuse angles paid off now as I confidently built the igloo, block by block.

I was so chilled that I had to concentrate on making my muscles function. With all the willpower I could muster, I hoisted block after block, finally lifting the last one into place. In less than an hour, the igloo was completed.

"How's it going?" I asked Sally as she tried to pack snow around the igloo, filling the cracks between blocks.

Sally said nothing. Instead, she raised a mitt-full of snow, and the fierce wind immediately blew the snow from her hand. I could see that it was an impossible task to paste snow into the cracks in such a wind.

"Let's just leave it," I said. We opened the tarp on the qamutik to dig out the things we needed for the night. There seemed to be as much snow inside the tarp as outside; fine grains had sifted into the canvas bags, stuff sacks, and even under the lids of the grub boxes.

Sally began hauling gear to the igloo while I retightened the lashings on the qamutik and checked for anything left in the snow. A shovel or snow knife would be buried within minutes, never to be found again.

Before retreating to the igloo, I had to feed the dogs. They wolfed down the frozen meat, then each dog curled into a ball and was promptly blanketed by snow.

"I've never seen a snowball grin before," Sally said as I crawled into the igloo. With her fingers, she melted the snow from my beard so that I could speak.

"What are you grinning about?" Sally asked.

"Oh, nothing much," I said, giving Sally a big hug and showering her with snow in the process. "It's just that here we are, in a real Arctic blizzard, in a real igloo, which we made with a real snow knife!" On this raw March day I should be wishing I was in a warm house, I thought, wriggling my toes to see whether they were still there. But, frozen though I was, I didn't want to be anywhere else.

"Today was the real test of everything Mamaaq has taught us," I said.

"And I think we did all right. It's pretty cozy in here!" Sally replied, warming her hands over the stove.

A pot of chicken glop was already bubbling on the stove. Sally and I were so hungry after our long day outdoors that we came a close second to the dogs in poor eating habits. We just spooned our supper straight from the pot.

"Ah yes, fine dining by the soft glow of a lantern," I said. Sally and I sat cross-legged on the caribou robe, facing each other with knees touching. The pot sat between us.

"It would be . . . if you didn't have your face in the pot!" Sally replied, laughing. I noticed she continued shovelling the food into her mouth as she talked. Mealtime etiquette was simple: the one who shovelled fastest ate the most. On average, we needed four to five thousand calories per day to keep warm, twice the normal daily requirement.

Our favourite suppers were affectionately called chicken glop and hamburger slop, each a mix of freeze-dried ingredients with rice or noodles. Another easy-to-prepare standby was macaroni and cheese, fortified with chunks of caribou meat. When we lived with Mamaaq, she had stressed the importance of eating meat to keep warm. A high meat diet raises the body's metabolic rate, keeping the internal furnace burning warmer. And we certainly needed all the warmth we could get.

Although the dogs could eat snow, we had to consume at least three litres of liquid a day to make up for moisture lost to the cold, dry air. Each morning we downed several cups of "high-fibre" tea, which featured caribou hairs floating on the surface—an unavoidable ingredient in our food and drink. We strained caribou-hair soup through our teeth at lunch, filled up with caribou-laced liquids at supper, and ended with a nightcap of fur-thickened hot chocolate.

With each pot of water tediously melted from ice or snow, precious liquid wasn't wasted on dish washing. After supper that night, I simply chipped snow off the igloo walls to scour the pot clean.

"It looks like we'll have tomato sauce in our cereal again tomorrow," I said, gazing at the frozen red residue in the pot.

"Hey, it adds colour to an otherwise boring bowl of hot cereal!" Sally declared.

Our evening chores completed, we removed our caribou clothing and wriggled into the sleeping bag. Crawling into an ice-cold bag that had been on the qamutik all day at minus thirty-five was the worst part of winter travel. I curled into a ball, groaning with disgust.

"Are you warm yet?" Sally asked through chattering teeth while moving closer to me. After what felt like the longest time, we stretched out as the bag slowly warmed. As Sally and I drifted off to sleep, we heard the muffled sounds of the storm and wondered how long it would last.

Storm-bound

The next morning, we pulled on our caribou-skin pants and atigis, which had been our pillows for the night. After weeks of wearing caribou clothing, we were beginning to look like caribou, and even smell like caribou. It was a musty, raw smell, but I reminded myself that the important thing was to keep warm. The caribou hairs were hollow and trapped air, giving the clothing remarkable insulating qualities.

When I pushed out the snow block at the doorway, snow swept into the igloo with an eager pounce. The scene outside was a white, swirling blur of snow. I couldn't even see the qamutik, a few steps from the door.

"I hope you find the accommodation to your liking," I said to Sally, quickly pushing the block back into place. "We're going to be here a while."

"You mean we get to spend the day in bed together? Sounds good to me!"

We were storm-bound. Sally and I snuggled down into our sleeping bag, happy to be together in the igloo without seven dogs competing for our attention. It was wonderful to relax and enjoy each other's company, to have a day off from the difficulties of winter travel. We spent the afternoon reading, playing cards, and sewing. I repaired Oonirgluk's harness, which he had gnawed when I hadn't removed it promptly. Sally stitched up holes in her caribou mitts that were a result of Kakpik's mischievous chewing the day before. Sally had removed her mitts to adjust Kakpik's harness, and he had been unable to resist the tantalizing sight of mitts dangling from the string around her neck.

"I wonder how the dogs are doing. Do you think we should bring them into the igloo?" Sally asked.

"Is this the same person who used to be afraid of dogs?" I said, laughing at the thought of seven unruly Huskies in the confines of the igloo.

I crawled outside to check on the dogs. The snow was coarse-grained, and it felt as if I was on the wrong side of a sandblasting machine. The grains of snow hissed loudly as they were blown across the ice, shifting, swirling, and constantly forming new drifts. Pulling the fur ruff of my parka tight around my face, I left a hole just large enough to peek out as I dug the dog food out of the qamutik.

Somehow in this maelstrom of snow, I had to find the dogs and feed them. Sally stood at the igloo holding one end of a rope, while I held the other and groped my way towards the mounds of snow that I hoped were the dogs. I was unable to see one foot in front of the other; no tracks showed where I passed.

"Here you go, Oonrigluk," I said, placing a chunk of seal meat beside him. He looked up from his hollow, too snug in his snow blanket to rise and greet me with his usual nudge with a shoulder. I worked my way along the stake-out chain, tossing a chunk of meat to each dog as I located him. The dogs looked quite comfortable and happily gnawed at their frozen meat.

Then I turned and fought my way back to the igloo. I called, but if Sally answered, I could not hear her over the wild howl of the wind. I held onto the rope tightly; only Sally would know if I became lost, and she would have little chance of finding me in the whiteout.

"Those boys sure are tough," I said to Sally after we had crawled back into the igloo. "They've each dug a cozy pit in the snow...except Tokak of course! He's either not too smart, or he's a lot tougher than the others."

High winds continued to sweep across the tundra the next morning. We lay under the caribou-fur blankets feeling restless, listening to the sound of the wind howling across the vent in the roof. I was thankful that we were in the igloo and not the tent.

By early afternoon, pinholes of light began to show on the windward side of the igloo. Driven by the wind, the coarse snow had cut through the softer snow of the wall. We patched the holes from the inside, but pinholes began to reappear before we'd finished our next card game. Reluctantly we headed outside and placed a row of blocks around the igloo. As I completed the blocks, Sally shovelled snow over the dome to seal it completely.

Waiting out a storm

Tokak after the snowstorm

191

The first day in the igloo had been a pleasant change from the routine of travelling. By the end of our second day, we had finished our only book, read the map, studied the first-aid manual, and memorized the freeze-dried food packages. While Sally sketched memories from days of dogsledding, I tried to recall impressions from our summer travels: the sounds of loons calling, waves lapping on a sandy beach, the smells of tundra flowers. I dug deep into my memory for special moments where all was not white and cold.

On our third storm-bound day, we began to feel a touch of claustrophobia, as though the white walls of the igloo were closing in on us. I longed to be outside, to be travelling again. Instead, I calculated how much dog food we had left. I worried about our fuel and supplies, which were dwindling rapidly. How long would the storm last? Would we have enough supplies to reach Arviat?

The wind diminished on the fourth day. Sally and I eagerly crawled out from the igloo, but our first view was intimidating. Snow drifts covered everything. The greyish white scene was illuminated by a ghostly glow in the white sky. There was no horizon, just white dimness. It was eerie, as if the entire world around us had been frozen in time.

Looking in the direction of the dogs, I saw only two noses and the tip of one ear poking out of the snow.

"Sally, help me dig the dogs out," I said, my voice tight with anxiety. We rushed over to where we had staked out the dogs and began digging, fearing the worst. I dug frantically, praying that our faithful travel companions hadn't suffocated under the snow.

Just below the surface we found Oonirgluk. He was quite snug and cozy in his form-fitting snow cave, insulated from the cold wind. Even though I dug away his shelter, he gave me a friendly nudge with his shoulder as he stood up.

Working down the chain, we dug out one dog at a time. Next came Kakpik, and Sally gave him a quick hug before we moved on to the next mound of snow. We cheered each time a dog stood up, tail wagging furiously. Every dog was alive! I was amazed that after enduring such a storm, the dogs simply shook the snow from their fur and were ready to go.

Although we had extricated the dogs from under the mantle of new snow, the qamutik was still buried under a deep drift. The wind had packed the snow so hard against the qamutik that Sally had to use our small axe to chop the drift into pieces before I could dig in with the shovel. Even so, I thought the shovel might break as I cleared away the snow. It took almost an hour to dig the qamutik out, and another half hour to free the stake-out chain.

"Ready?" I asked Sally as I finally hooked the last dog to his lead line. The dogs were certainly ready and eager to run after their three-day rest.

Sally nodded, preoccupied with her task of holding the squirming dogs. A moment later, Kakpik escaped from her grasp.

"Okay!" Sally said, releasing the others. As I pulled up the snow hook, the dogs surged forward. Sally scrambled out of their way, jumping onto the qamutik as it sped past.

The first fifteen minutes were as fast and furious as ever. As the dogs slowed to their all-day trot, we scanned the changed, cloud-scudded horizon.

"It looks so different after the storm. Without the sun I'd have no idea which to go!" Sally said.

"Me neither," I confessed.

I studied the snowscape, looking for a landmark, any landmark. There was no delineation between the flat sea ice and the flat land. I checked the time and the position of the sun, then turned my attention back to the dogs. Oonirgluk was leaning eagerly into the wind, running southwest down the coast.

"No problem," I said. "Now that Oonrigluk is pointed in the right direction, he'll keep going that way!"

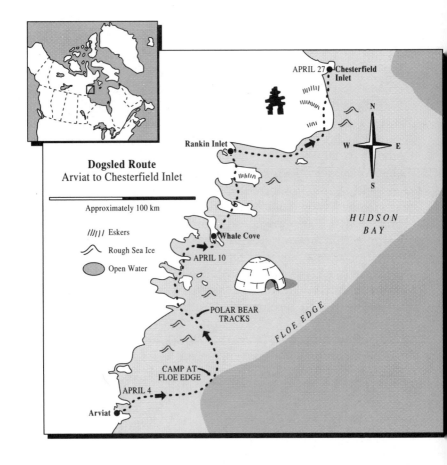

Dogsled Route
Arviat to Chesterfield Inlet

Approximately 100 km

////|/ Eskers

Rough Sea Ice

Open Water

APRIL 27 Chesterfield Inlet

Rankin Inlet

Whale Cove

APRIL 10

POLAR BEAR TRACKS

CAMP AT FLOE EDGE

APRIL 4

Arviat

HUDSON BAY

FLOE EDGE

N
W E
S

E I G H T E E N

Qimuksiq

"Come on, boys," I urged as we neared Arviat a few days after the storm. "Extra rations if we get there tonight!"

More than five hundred kilometres of ice and snow had passed under the runners of our qamutik since leaving Chesterfield Inlet. After travelling for three weeks, and surviving two dog fights and seven storms, we now felt confident at *qimuksiq* (dogsledding).

Sally and I staked out the dogs just off the sea ice then wandered through the hamlet of Arviat. It was about the same size as Baker Lake, an isolated community of only twelve hundred people. The first person we saw was a man planing the runners of a small qamutik. He introduced himself as Muckpah, and while he continued working we told him where we had come from.

"Come in for tea," Muckpah said as he finished planing the runner. As with everyone else we had visited, "tea" meant sharing whatever food was in the house. Although we had become used to this generous northern hospitality, it still felt very special to be invited into the home of someone we had only just met.

Muckpah spoke English, though it was well punctuated with Inuktitut words.

"Not many people travel by qimuksiq anymore," he said, pushing the teapot our way. He paused reflectively, looking out the window towards the sea ice. After several minutes of silence, he asked where we were going next.

"We're heading back to Chesterfield Inlet, then north along the coast for another month."

"Maybe I should go with you for a few days," he said, his eyes lighting up. He talked about dogsledding to the floe edge and looking for seals and polar bears near the open water.

"That would be great!" I said. "We've always wanted to go to the floe edge." Sally and I had never ventured to where the sea ice meets the open water; it was too dangerous to go there with our lack of knowledge about the ever-changing ice conditions.

In preparation for the trip, Muckpah showed us how to make kamiks to protect the dogs' feet from the sharp sea ice near the floe edge. We watched carefully as he cut a rectangular piece of canvas and pierced two holes for the middle claws to poke through. He also suggested we bring a plastic tarp to put under our caribou furs. The ice at the floe edge, he explained, was salty and would ruin the caribou skins.

On the morning of our departure, Sally and I were busy harnessing the dogs when we heard a whistle. I looked up and saw Muckpah racing across the sea ice with ten dogs pulling his qamutik. Close behind him was another dog team. The qamutiks looked odd and I squinted across the snow to study them. A small wooden boat was lashed to each sled—a strange sight in the middle of winter. The men reclined comfortably in the boats as their Huskies raced across the frozen white landscape.

We caught up with Muckpah and the other dog-teamer, Panegoniak, when they stopped for a tea break. Surrounded by a clutter of gear, Muckpah tended to a kettle of tea brewing on the stove. Panegoniak was busy slicing off meat from a haunch of caribou. Bannock and a box of biscuits were laid out on the snow.

Sally and I dug out our food and joined the men. We munched on our usual lunch of hard biscuits with frozen slices of salami and cheese, washed down with instant soup. While I sipped my soup, I kept an eye on the dogs. They were lying obediently in the snow, but I didn't fully trust them to remain there.

"Kimmiq!" I said sternly when he became restless. The tone of my voice was enough to make him settle down. I tried to act unconcerned about our team's behaviour, but secretly I worried that they might start chewing each other up in front of our travel companions. Luckily, all our efforts over the last two weeks to make the dogs behave paid off—the entire tea break passed without incident.

We had been lagging behind because of our heavy load, so Muckpah offered to take Sally on his qamutik. He cleared a spot for her in the boat, pushing aside a grub box, tent poles, paddles, and cans of campstove fuel. Sally made herself comfortable on the tent and a bundle of caribou furs.

Now I was able to keep up with the others. This was the ultimate northern experience! A year ago, I wouldn't have imagined myself driving my own dog team in the company of two Inuit and their teams.

"Your wife, she must be heavy!" Muckpah called to me when Oonirgluk pulled out to pass his team.

As the qamutik jostled across the ice, Muckpah stood in his boat and studied the route ahead through binoculars. He pointed to a passage through the upheaved ice, then led the way to the floe edge. It was hard work for the dogs and drivers as the sleds twisted and tipped at precarious angles over high pressure ridges of ice.

I held my breath, my heart beating loudly as the sled crossed thin-looking ice that led to the floe edge. Muckpah stopped only metres from the sea. The endless white we had been looking at for weeks and weeks ended at the vast expanse of black open water.

Sunlight sparkled on the dark water, contrasting vividly

The team running flat out

Sally and the team by an igloo

with the white ice at the floe edge. Where the ice was driven into ten-metre-high piles, we saw shades of icy blue, so brilliant it seemed the blocks of ice were illuminated from within.

"Maybe we'll camp here," Muckpah said.

"Here?" Sally asked, glancing nervously at the open water. We had heard stories of the ice shearing off near the floe edge, leaving hunters drifting out to sea. Muckpah and Panegoniak are okay, I thought to myself; they have boats.

They stood confidently at the edge of the ice. Even so, Sally and I felt uneasy and couldn't believe we were going to pitch our tents so close to the open water. I wondered how we would chain out the dogs and pitch our tent on the bare ice.

"Let's take our time and see what they do," I suggested.

Nearby were pressure ridges with an unlimited supply of large chunks of ice. These, it turned out, were an ideal place to secure the dog chains. Muckpah tied each end of his stake-out chain around a car-sized block of ice and tethered the dogs for the night. Then he carried smaller chunks of ice to his campsite and tied his tent ropes to them.

Although Muckpah set up his tent only two strides from the dark ocean, we set up ours ten metres away. Since leaving Chesterfield, we had been travelling on the snow-covered sea ice, but usually within sight of land. Except when the ice trembled beneath us, it had always seemed as though we were on firm ground . . . until now.

"Do you feel the ice moving?" Sally asked in a whisper, moving close to me.

"Nope," I said nonchalantly. "You probably haven't got your land legs yet after racing around in Muckpah's boat all day."

Then Sally drew my attention to the edge of the ice, which was rising and falling with the waves. The movement was barely perceptible but alarming. As I watched the ice move, I couldn't shake the thought that if a violent wind came up, the ice under us would crumble and we would be fish food.

As soon as they had finished camp chores, Panegoniak and

Muckpah set out to look for seals. Carrying his long harpoon, Muckpah walked along the edge of the ice. Panegoniak was more cautious and pushed his qamutik along the ice. His boat was still on the sled, so if he fell through the ice he could climb into the boat. Unfortunately the men saw no seals. Panegoniak would have to manage without the fresh meat he had counted on for the journey to Whale Cove with Sally and me.

"I'd like to go anyway," he said. "Muckpah will give me some meat. And maybe we'll see caribou on the way."

"We have some extra dog food," I volunteered, pleased that he wanted to go with us.

Later that evening, all four of us crowded into Muckpah's canvas tent. Muckpah looked comfortable, stretched out on his stomach while he tended a pot of caribou meat that was simmering on the stove. Within reach was everything he needed for his meal: tea, bannock, and a hunting knife. Panegoniak watched from his bag and lay propped up on an elbow, sipping tea. One candle illuminated the tent with a soft, warm glow.

Inuktitut was the language they were most comfortable with, but Panegoniak, who was in his mid-thirties, spoke English fairly well. He helped Muckpah translate a word now and then as they talked about their favourite dogs, dogsledding, and travel on the sea ice.

"Sea ice is different from lake ice," Muckpah told us. "One foot might go through or the ice might sag, but sea ice doesn't break under you like lake ice. If the sea ice is thin, go like a polar bear and crawl," he continued.

"Like this?" I asked.

Muckpah burst into laughter at the sight of me crab-walking around with my hands and feet spread wide.

"No, like this," he said, rising to his hands and knees. "You have to grunt like a bear too!" Once Muckpah had stopped laughing, we learned that crawling distributes a person's weight over a wider area and lessens the chance of breaking through the ice.

Walking back to our tent late in the evening, Sally and

I stopped to look over the camp: three dog teams and qamutiks, and two canvas tents at the edge of the sea ice. The scene was illuminated by the soft glow of moonlight. Long shadows stretched from the tents and followed the contours of the snow.

"There's nowhere else I'd rather be," I said to Sally, the vapour from my words floating in the cold night air. Standing together, we cast one long shadow across the snow. We stood in silence for several minutes, absorbing the beauty and stillness of the Arctic night before continuing to our tent.

The next morning, we woke to loud cracking noises vibrating through the ice underneath us.

Kkk-rrr-aak! Kkk-rrr-aak! Every few seconds a report echoed across the ice.

"The ice!" Sally exclaimed. We looked at each other, thinking exactly the same thing: we were doomed.

I peered out of the tent door, expecting the worst.

"It's okay," I reported back to Sally, then chuckled at our nervousness. "It's just Muckpah testing the new ice with his harpoon."

New ice had formed overnight and Muckpah was walking across it. Every three or four steps, he jabbed his harpoon into the ice. Although his harpoon went through the ice on every jab, certain places must have been thinner than others because he made many detours.

Sally looked over my shoulder for a moment. "I can't watch!" she said, when the ice sagged under Muckpah. "I'm sure he'll break through."

I continued watching, spellbound, until Muckpah was just a speck on the horizon.

"No seals today," Muckpah said when he came back from his walk. Muckpah decided to return to Arviat. Panegoniak was still optimistic about seeing caribou on the way to Whale Cove, so he decided to continue with us.

Panegoniak led the way, but most of the time he was merely a black speck in the distance. With tracks to follow, Oonirgluk needed little guidance. I enjoyed the chance to

Untangling the lead lines

Camping on the sea ice

talk with Sally without having to watch the dogs' every movement. The steady, rocking motion of the sled lulled me to a state of inattention.

I was jolted back to reality when Tokak collapsed on the snow. It happened so fast a qamutik rail ran over his tail and one leg. Tokak didn't utter a sound.

"Whoa," I commanded and pushed the snow hook into the snow with all my strength.

"Help me lift the qamutik off him!" I called anxiously. Tokak was still breathing, but he lay flattened on the snow, ears back, and eyes closed tightly. He was trembling slightly and breathed though his nose with quick, shallow breaths as if trying not to make a sound. I had never seen any of the dogs act this way before.

At first I thought Tokak was injured. Then I noticed a huge track in the snow, larger than two of my mittened hands. Polar bear! The track was so fresh that the blowing snow had not yet filled it in. Nervously, I looked over my shoulder. Tokak looked nervously over his.

How difficult would it be to spot a white bear on the white snow? A shiver crept down my spine.

I talked to Tokak in a low, reassuring voice, and stroked his head. After a few minutes, I managed to persuade him that there was nothing to worry about, and he rejoined the team.

"Did you see the polar bear tracks?" Panegoniak asked us when we caught up with him.

"We sure did! Our toughest dog collapsed into a pile of trembling fur when we came to them."

We built an igloo for the night when the storm that had been brewing all day finally caught up with us. The igloo was a small shelter for the three of us, so we brought in the minimum of supplies—one grub box, one lantern, pots, supper, and breakfast. After we had one last visit outside, Panegoniak secured the entrance for the night. He picked up a mittful of soft snow and pasted the snow around the edges of the snow block, sealing it shut.

In the morning, Panegoniak slid his snow knife around the

snow block at the doorway, then pushed the block out. It had been so quiet inside, we were surprised to see a howling blizzard.

"Oh well, we can sleep," Panegoniak said cheerfully. We wouldn't be travelling.

As the hours passed, we got to know Panegoniak better. He talked about his early days of sledding and told of his problems when he first started. We compared stories of runaway teams, fur-flying fights, and other near-disasters, but we agreed there was no better way to travel than by dog team, despite the problems.

"My dogs are much better than a Ski-doo," Panegoniak said. "They don't break down, and they'll even run on an empty tank!"

The next morning the weather had cleared only a little, but we decided to push on. Two more days of travel brought us to Whale Cove, where we picked up more supplies. Panegoniak was stopping here, so we said farewell to our travel companion.

"Maybe I'll see caribou on the way back!" he said, the eternal optimist. In a land so harsh and with weather and animal sightings so fickle, perhaps one always has to be optimistic.

Sally and I continued north towards Chesterfield Inlet. Travel was easy across the windblown snow, and the dogs covered a lot of ground each day with their long, steady stride.

Fourteen days, one minor dog skirmish, and two snow-storms later, we spied a mass of grey cloud on the horizon. This was the characteristic "water sky," a cloud that always hangs over the open water near Chesterfield Inlet.

That night we talked about the next part of our journey. It was now the end of April, and there were almost eighteen hours of daylight each day. Compared to the frigid days of March, the minus-ten degree temperatures seemed almost tropical. With the long days and ideal travel conditions, we were eager to go exploring even further north.

We sat in the tent, with maps spread out across the

caribou blanket, and talked about the uncertainties of the route and the logistics of carrying enough supplies for a month-long trip. Sally and I looked forward to seeing new country and to the challenges ahead. But first we had to cut 140 toenails and trim the fur from 28 paws.

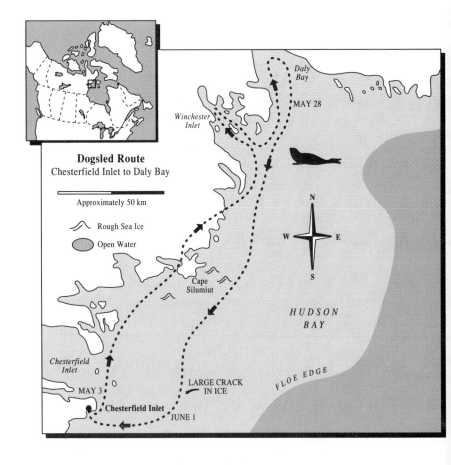

Dogsled Route
Chesterfield Inlet to Daly Bay

Approximately 50 km

～へ Rough Sea Ice

◯ Open Water

Daly
Bay

MAY 28

Winchester
Inlet

N
W ✦ E
S

Cape
Silumiut

HUDSON
BAY

Chesterfield
Inlet

MAY 3

Chesterfield Inlet

LARGE CRACK
IN ICE

JUNE 1

FLOE EDGE

N I N E T E E N

Exploring

"Kakpik...whoa, whoa!" I held a squirming, whining bundle of energy while Sally trimmed the fur between the pads of Kakpik's feet. This ticklish task was necessary because clumps of sun-softened snow stuck to the long hair on the dogs' feet when they ran, causing them to limp.

Then Sally clipped Kakpik's toenails—all twenty of them. Long toenails, useful in soft snow, were now a hindrance. They often broke on the icy crust that formed when the melting snow froze again each night.

We moved on to Tokak, who enjoyed the attention, and merely tried to lick me as Sally cut his fur and trimmed his nails. Predictably, Kimmiq was the most difficult, jumping, twisting, and turning as I tried to hold him down. Two hours and twenty-eight feet later, we had finally finished all the dogs.

"Lucky we have only seven dogs!" an exhausted Sally said. Now we were ready to go exploring.

Although we already had more than a thousand kilometres under the qamutik runners, Sally and I looked forward to this new adventure. We felt we had finally mastered dogsledding and felt confident venturing farther north, where no settlements existed.

We continued north along the coast on May 3. As soon as we crossed Chesterfield Inlet, the curving coastline became more rugged and broken. There were endless bays, inlets, and small islands—all similar, making it difficult for us to pinpoint our location.

The dogs ran shoulder to shoulder in tight formation, working well as a team. I called "Howa-ii," and the team obediently turned to the right. One nudge from Sally, standing at the rear push-bar, and the qamutik followed in a smooth arc.

The days blended together with the rhythm of our nomadic life. From the harnessing of dogs each morning to the setting up of our camp each evening, we had developed a well-tuned routine. The dogs also knew our routine after two months of travel. At the end of each day, they sprawled in the snow, seemingly asleep, but monitoring our activities with twitching ears.

"They know what's next," I said when we walked towards the qamutik after setting up camp one evening. As Sally opened a canvas bag, every dog stood up, looking at us in anticipation.

When the dogs saw me pull out two large pots for soaking the dried food, they understood that there would be a delay. Melting snow for water and soaking the food took almost an hour. Each time we lifted a lid to stir the contents, there was an unavoidable soft chink of metal on metal, and the dogs jerked to attention.

Seven tired, quiet dogs turned into howling, snapping, lunging beasts when I emerged from the tent bearing two pails of dog food. It was supper time!

I always worried that the four stakes anchoring the chain would be wrenched from the snow. After all, each dog was capable of pulling fifty to seventy kilograms all day long. My control of the dogs evaporated at feeding time, when they went completely berserk.

Sally and I worked fast to minimize the lunging. We fed

Oonirgluk first to reinforce his position as boss dog, and the rest of the team followed in order of rank on the fan hitch. By the time we reached Kimmiq at the end of the line, he was leaping against his chain with wild abandon.

From feeding the dogs each night to handling them throughout the day, Sally and I now worked well together, confident in our own tasks. Whenever a dog became tangled or began to limp because of ice in a paw, I would stop the team; Sally would then run to the dogs. They always stood quietly and waited while Sally aided the dog with a problem. I don't know whether it was because she never disciplined them or because she had a gentler touch, but they seemed to understand what she wanted and would cooperate.

Congratulating ourselves on how smoothly our trip was going, we crossed a long stretch of land to avoid rough sea ice one afternoon. As we headed down one of the steep, boulder-strewn eskers, Sally rode at the back, dragging a snow hook to keep the sled from running over the dogs.

Suddenly the sled stopped as abruptly as if we had run into a brick wall. The dogs were jerked backwards off their feet; I tumbled off the sled; and Sally lay sprawled in the snow beside the snow hook.

"Neat trick, eh?" Sally said, laughing. Then she explained that the snow hook had caught on a rock under the snow. I thought back to our first weeks with the team. If this had happened then, I probably would have accused Sally of carelessness, and she would have been in tears, anticipating a fur-flying dog fight. Now we laughed at the incident, and as soon as I lifted the whip, each dog lay down.

The force of the sudden stop had snapped the rope that attached the sled to the lead lines. Only the day before we had cut the spare rope to use for something else! We patched the tow rope as best as we could and headed on our way again.

Our sense of humour was tested several more times as we continued overland. Ptarmigan frequently burst from the willows, causing the dogs to lurch sideways and give chase.

It was futile to try to stop them, and I finally let them follow their instincts.

"Go get 'em, Oonirgluk," I urged as Sally and I began to enjoy this new diversion as much as the dogs.

Each day the sun arced higher in the sky, and daylight lasted longer into the evening. The temperature still averaged minus ten degrees, but the sun now had noticeable warmth to it. During the middle of the day, the temperature often became warm enough for us to remove our toques— the toques we had worn day and night for almost three months. Now we enjoyed the simple, almost forgotten pleasure of the wind ruffling our hair.

The brilliance of the spring sun reflecting on the snow was so acute that snow goggles were essential. Without them, we knew snow blindness could occur in a matter of hours.

"You're looking awfully red," I said to Sally one afternoon. Her face looked as though she'd been sunning herself in Hawaii.

"You too," she replied, removing her snow goggles for a better look at me.

How could we be sunburnt? Each morning we coated our cheeks and noses with gobs of sunscreen even before we left the tent. Several times a day we slapped on more lotion.

We looked at each other's lobster-red features, then scrambled for the bottle of sunscreen.

"Take a look at the fine print," Sally said, handing me the bottle.

On the back, in very tiny letters, it said *"Caution: Do not freeze."*

The long days of sunlight also warmed the water that had flooded up between cracks at high tide. The seawater no longer froze, but sat in aquamarine puddles on the white ice. Oonirgluk led the team in a zigzag route to avoid stepping in the water. When the dogs had no choice but to cross the salty slush, their paws became clogged with snow as soon as they stepped back on the dry snow. Many times we had to stop and let them chew out the lumps before continuing.

"I know what you're thinking, Tokak," Sally said when he

lay down in the snow and looked at her. "Chew your own ice lumps!"

In addition to the puddles of water, there were now many cracks across the sea ice. At first we didn't pay any attention to the thin fissures in the snow—we'd seen them all winter—but after one runner of the sled fell into a large, hidden crack, we did our best to keep clear of any cracks. If we had to cross them, we did so by running straight across.

We began to see seals about the time water-filled cracks appeared. The sea ice was dotted with black forms of seals that had climbed through the gaps to bask in the warm sun. When a seal caught our scent, it lumbered to the crack and slid down into the safety of the water.

Whenever the dogs smelled a seal, they picked up their pace. The most eager was Anukti, who ran with his head held high, sniffing in the direction of the seals.

"Anukti!" I yelled, just before he crashed into a block of ice, bowling him off his feet.

"He never learns!" Sally said, shaking her head as he regained his balance and joined the others. He was so intent on watching the seals that he continued to stumble or crash into obstacles each time we came across a black form on the ice.

As we came around a pressure ridge one afternoon, we saw a seal fast asleep on the ice. The dogs lurched forward, nearly doubling their speed. We were downwind, and the dogs approached in silence, with the stealth of hunters.

The dogs took us closer and closer until we could see every whisker on the seal's face. The seal was the same length as I am, but it was so bulky I wouldn't have been able to wrap my arms around it.

I studied the animal for a moment, then realized we were almost upon it. I imagined the terrible scene if the seven dogs had a chance to attack.

"Hey!" I yelled to the inert mammal. In a split second it dived into the crack. I'd never have thought such a rotund animal could move that quickly.

That afternoon, I was less strict with the dogs and let

them enjoy themselves, running flat out across the ice every time they saw or smelled a seal. As long as they pulled us in the general direction we wanted to go, I let them veer off course for the fun of the chase. After all, even dogs can catch spring fever.

This was a northern spring at its best. Sally and I lounged together on the sled soaking up the warmth of the sun. We lay back on the qamutik, resting on a comfortable bed of caribou furs.

"Ah, this is the life," I mused, watching seven wagging tails and twenty-eight feet as the qamutik thumped across the ice. The dogs ran with new-found energy, tongues lolling out of their mouths and feet flying over the snow. This idyllic mode of travel was marred only by sitting downwind from the back end of seven Huskies that had been dining on fish for days.

Day after day, the dogs pulled us steadily northward. Twenty kilometres, a daily goal that had seemed almost impossible in the soft snow of March, was now a short day of easy travel.

Now and then we saw inukshuks, a sign that others had travelled this way before. They were probably built decades ago, when Inuit had travelled along the coast by dog team, as we were travelling now. As the wind howled across the ice, I imagined that I heard the howling of long-past teams. After months of travel, I felt that I knew what the people of this vast land had experienced many years ago. Although we had some modern equipment with us, the daily routine of dogsled travel had changed little. It was still the age-old interdependence of humans and dogs.

Sally and I decided to take a break from travelling when we came to a small island topped with three inukshuks. Just below these rock cairns, a meadow carpeted with heather had emerged from the snow.

It looked like an ideal place to camp for a few days. Using blocks of snow, we built an easy chair for two near the tent. We relaxed with a caribou blanket tucked around us, and the dogs sprawled out on the snow, also enjoying a

Mending a dog harness

Supper time at a spring camp

siesta. This was Arctic paradise: a calm day with the sun shimmering across the glazed snow.

Below the horizon was a sparkling white world, and above, the sky was tinted an intense cobalt blue by my snow goggles. An island in the distance, the only visible landmark on the ice, was a small bump on the blue line between sea ice and sky.

"The freshness, the freedom, the farness," Sally said, quoting the words of Robert Service as we looked over the vast landscape. We no longer felt overwhelmed by the openness the way we had when we first came north. We had come to terms with the land's vastness and our smallness.

It was after eight when we started supper that night, cooking outside the tent to make the most of the sunshine. Even though we had already fed the dogs, they sat looking at us expectantly—they were downwind from the tantalizing smells coming from our pots!

Several days of warm weather forced us to change our travel routine. By the third week of May, we could no longer travel midday because the snow was too soft. We had to start travelling late each afternoon, when the snow had become firm.

With long daylight hours, we often ran late into the night. By nine o'clock one evening, the sun was low and each dog cast a ten-metre-long shadow featuring amazingly long legs. Sally and I became pencil-thin giants riding on the qamutik.

While the dogs pulled us across the ice, the sun turned to crimson as it sank towards the skyline. The sun warmed the scene with a rosy glow as it melted over the horizon. We set up camp an hour later, in the half-light of dusk.

"Don't get snow downwind from the dogs," Sally advised as I collected snow for water. They were shedding, and the wind blew their fine winter underfur onto the snow. The hairs were invisible until we found them floating in our soup or tea!

Just after midnight, we went out for a last check on the dogs before turning in. There was still some pink reflected on a band of clouds just above the western horizon. Best of all, in the pale light over the tent, northern lights danced.

Long bands of light darted down towards the horizon, and behind them shifting curtains of green and white danced across the sky. This time of year, even the northern lights seemed warm, the coloured waves soft and pulsing.

"I guess that means a change of weather," I said to Sally as we watched the cosmic light show above us.

We woke the next morning to the pattering of rain on the canvas tent. Rain! Water dripped off the roof, the air was mild, and birds were singing. It was if winter had ended overnight. Sally and I lay in the tent listening to the rain and the watery, warbling song of snow buntings. Almost eight months had passed since the temperature had last been above freezing. It was May 24 and spring had finally arrived on the coast of Hudson Bay.

Spring Thaw

After two days of rain, a patchwork of meltwater spread across the surface of the ice, forming blue ponds on a sea of white.

"Time to put away the caribou clothes. It's going to be a wet ride," I said to Sally. We changed into rubber boots and waterproof rain pants and parkas for the day.

The rain-softened snow meant we had to get back to Chesterfield Inlet as soon as possible. Even if the snow did not become too slushy for travel and the dogs pulled hard, it would still take more than a week to reach Chesterfield Inlet.

Waves of water washed over the front of the sled and splashed up from the dogs' feet as they high-stepped through the puddles. In some places, the water was so deep the qamutik sank to the top of the crossbars and lost all momentum. The dogs enjoyed running through the puddles though, lapping up water as they went. After the deepest puddles, they slowed momentarily to shake out their fur, then continued running.

When we took a shortcut across a peninsula, we found the

sun had melted the snow, revealing large patches of rock and tundra. Heather crushed by the qamutik runners filled the air with a fragrant aroma. Less welcome than the heather, however, were the rocks that ground against the runners. We decided that we would have to take the long route back to Chesterfield Inlet, following the sea ice.

Travelling across the sea ice had also become more challenging. By the end of May, the cracks in the ice had grown considerably wider.

"It looks cold and dark down there," I mused, looking at the seawater as the sled thumped over one of the cracks. Each day we crossed many cracks in the ice, first visible as dark lines on the white snow. While I directed the dogs, Sally stood at the back of the qamutik, scanning for wide cracks.

As we neared Chesterfield Inlet, we saw another black line indicating an open crack.

"Go left!" Sally called from her high viewpoint at the push-bar.

"Hulla, hulla," I translated, but Oonirgluk had seen the crack and was already turning so that the dogs would run straight across the gap. We were only two qamutik-lengths away when I realized that this crack was different—it was more than one metre wide! The dogs were speeding up to jump the gap. We were nearly upon it, and I had a sickening feeling that we might not make it across.

I braced myself and hoped for the best.

Oonirgluk, Kakpik, and Anukti cleared the crack. We watched in horror as the next four dogs plunged into the black, icy water.

"Brake!" I yelled to Sally, even though we both knew the snow hook wouldn't work on the ice. I could hear the frantic scraping of metal on ice from Sally's snow hook. At the last possible moment, the hook caught on something and the qamutik jerked to a stop. The front of the qamutik was suspended over the water.

Tokak had managed to scramble onto the ice, but the other dogs were paddling furiously in the frigid water and clawing at the ice. They were unable to climb out.

The dogs were beginning to panic and I had to work quickly. While Sally stood on the snow hook to keep the sled from being pulled forward, I rushed to the edge of the crack. I reached over and grabbed Arnako's harness. He was paddling the water in terror, looking at me with eyes wide with fear.

"It's okay, boy," I murmured, trying to calm the both of us. I hauled the water-soaked dog up onto the ice.

I'd spoken too soon. With a sickening *crack!* the ice gave way beneath us. Arnako and I plunged into the near-freezing water.

"Ian!" I heard Sally scream. Frantically, I kicked my way across the gap with water-filled boots. Dogs were churning the water around me.

I struggled to heave myself onto the ice beside the dogs that had made it across. Oonirgluk whimpered as I tried to climb out, grasping for a hand-hold on the slippery surface. On my third attempt, the front of the qamutik slid by me— Sally had pushed the sled across the gap, forming a bridge. I reached up and grabbed a crossbar. With a desperate kick, I flopped onto the ice.

Lying flat on the ice, I reached for the harness nearest me and pulled Arnako from the water. This time, with my weight spread out, the ice didn't break. I reached out for another soggy creature.

"Come on, Kimmiq," I urged as he struggled to climb out.

Knowing that Kimmiq was likely to tangle all the lead lines, I pushed him across the qamutik to Sally. She tied him to the back of the sled to keep him out of the way.

"Can you...get...Tuaa?" I said, through chattering teeth. "I can't...reach him!" Exhausted, Tuaa sagged in the water with only his chin resting on the ice.

Sally lay on her stomach and pulled on his harness. She struggled to pull Tuaa out, but he was tangled in the other dogs' traces. Each time those dogs moved, they pulled Tuaa away from the edge of the ice.

"Keep the dogs still!" shouted Sally, exasperated.

I couldn't. They were too upset and were beginning to snap at each other. As best I could, I held onto Tokak, Anukti, and Kakpik.

Sally plunged an arm into the icy water and unwrapped the lines from Tuaa's legs and stomach. Then, using all her strength, she hauled him out. Tuaa was trembling violently, probably as much from the shock as the cold.

Like Tuaa, I was shivering with cold and nervous tension as I contemplated the difficult task ahead. Somehow, I had to coerce, haul, push, or prod five dogs across the qamutik bridge back to the other side. One by one, I shoved the reluctant dogs towards Sally. With plenty of coaxing from Sally, they crept timidly across.

When Arnako's turn came, he wouldn't move. Finally I picked him up and carried him across. The qamutik, narrow and still packed with all our equipment, was not an easy bridge to cross.

"Tokak!" I heard Sally shout. I looked up long enough to see that Tokak and Anukti had attacked Tuaa. Any weak dog was fair game, especially when the dogs were so upset.

With strength that surprised me, Sally held Tokak with one hand and pulled Anukti off with the other. The rest of the dogs were beginning to growl and snap at each other, a release of tension.

"Let's get out of here before they have a fight," Sally urged as I stepped off the qamutik onto the ice. Although I was cold and my clothing was wet, I agreed. We had to run the dogs to dry them off and calm them down.

As soon as I turned the sled, Sally let go of the dogs and I gave the command to go. I breathed a sigh of relief when all seven dogs leaned into their harnesses and pulled away.

For almost half an hour, we ran the dogs. It was just what they needed; each dog pulled hard as if nothing had happened. Oonrigluk and the team had always amazed us with their strength and stamina. Today they impressed us with their courage and fortitude. I wanted to give each dog a big hug of thanks, but that would have to wait until the end of the day.

"You look cold," Sally said. "I can hold the dogs while you change." The wind was cutting through my water-soaked clothing, chilling me to the bone.

"Whoa," I called to the team. As soon as the dogs came to a halt, they lay down and began licking the saltwater from their fur.

While I changed into dry clothes, Sally checked the dogs.

"His fur is dry," Sally said with obvious relief as she ran her fingers through Tuaa's fur. Even though he had been in the water for many minutes, his soft underfur was warm and dry.

"The dogs deserve an extra ration this evening," I said, looking over to the team.

"You could use some extra rations too!" Sally said. "I think there's some extra chocolate in the grub box."

We continued on for another two hours until we reached a small island. Only when we had chained out the dogs and set up camp did we have time to talk about the experience.

"It was like a nightmare watching you floundering with the dogs," Sally said, clenching her mug of tea tightly. "I knew if I let go of the snow hook and went to help you, the dogs would pull the sled into the water. All I could do was slide the qamutik towards you."

Our eyes met over our dinners. We were both thinking the same thing, I was sure. We had learned, again, that we could count on each other in any emergency.

"You did a great job," I said quietly.

"You too," Sally smiled. Then she laughed with a release of tension. "Now I know why Muckpah had a boat on his qamutik!"

I hoped we wouldn't need a boat. Even though we were still thirty kilometres from Chesterfield Inlet, we felt we should push to get there in one day. The ice was too treacherous for us to travel even one extra day.

As we settled under the caribou blanket, I listened to the soothing sounds of rustling dogs and clinking chains in the night. Kimmiq growled softly, and I heard another dog shake himself, his chain rattling a syncopated rhythm.

Anukti during hookup!   *Oonirgluk howling*

A wet ride through meltwater

221

"Life will seem pretty quiet without the team," I said.

Sally and I planned to canoe south as soon as the sea ice melted, and we couldn't take the dogs with us. When we had passed through Chesterfield Inlet a month earlier, Eli had asked if he could have the team back when we were finished. Until then we had worried about finding a good home for the dogs.

The next morning, we loaded the qamutik and pulled the snow hooks out of the soft snow for the final time. As they had every day during our trip, the dogs leaned eagerly into their harnesses and pulled away. Sally and I reflected on how far we had come with the dogs—not just in distance travelled, but in our relationship with the team. With feelings of sadness, we watched the last day of our dogsled journey slide by.

When we reached Chesterfield Inlet, we took the dogs back to Eli. Sally and I would miss our seven canine companions. They had been the source of both our greatest pleasures and most frustrating moments. We had been with them twenty-four hours a day for months. Each dog—even Kimmiq—had become a special friend to us. But we knew they belonged here, where they could run, pull a qamutik, and chase after seals.

I patted Oonirgluk for the last time, then Kakpik, Arnako, Anukti, Tokak, Tuaa, and Kimmiq. Sally fussed over each dog, then buried her face in Kakpik's fur.

I felt a lump rise in my throat, and had trouble speaking. "Goodbye, boys," I said quietly.

As we walked away, the dogs began to howl. Every time we had disappeared from the dogs' sight in the past months they had done the same. They had no way of knowing that this time we were not coming back.

First Oonirgluk, then Kakpik, and then all the others joined in a chorus. It began as a high-pitched medley and dropped to a melancholy-sounding wail. All muzzles were pointed to the sky, lips pursed as they howled their dog-song. Then suddenly, as if on cue, they stopped and all was silent.

On the Land

We woke to the drumroll of pebbles bouncing down the roof of our tent. Every few seconds, a rattle vibrated across the taut canvas, making it impossible to sleep.

Suddenly the door of the tent burst open. A small impish face peered in.

"Leroy, we're trying to sleep!" I pleaded, then heard the patter of feet as the six-year-old boy retreated to his tent.

Sally and I were camped among a cluster of white, weather-worn canvas tents near Chesterfield Inlet. Early June is "back to the land" time for the Inuit, when many families leave their houses to spend much of the summer at tent camps. A few days earlier, we had joined the camp and pitched our tent beside Leroy's family, the Kukkiaks, while we waited for the sea ice to melt.

From our tent, we heard the deep voices of men returning from a hunting trip, followed shortly after by the metallic ring of ulus being sharpened against rocks. That sound told us that the hunt had been successful. When we ventured out half an hour later, we saw Papaluk Kukkiak cutting caribou meat into thin slices to dry in the sun. Bright orange-red strips of Arctic char, caught on previous outings, were also drying in the warm breeze.

It was a busy time of year. The camp echoed with the sounds of children playing tag or wrestling with puppies. Babies, who had hardly been outdoors all winter, bounced about in amautis worn by their older sisters. Children wearing hip waders or knee-high rubber boots wandered across the soggy tundra gathering eggs.

"Can you come egg hunting?" Leroy asked one morning.

We abandoned our chores and accompanied Leroy and his cousins across the tundra. Ponds nearby echoed with the distinctive call of the oldsquaw ducks and the croak of red-throated loons. From the shoreline came the soft call of plovers and a symphony of other sounds. Creeks, which were still frozen only a week earlier, had come to life, dancing between boulders. The air was rich with the scents of musty, wet soil and fragrant new flowers.

We copied the children and walked with heads down, peering into every shaded depression. The most difficult eggs to find were the oldsquaw eggs, we learned.

"The mothers cover the eggs with moss and grass so you can't see them," Diane told us.

"Ian, come look!" Leroy called. Tucked under an over-hanging rock, he had found a nest of tiny eggs.

"Over here," Diane urged, when she found a nest filled with eider eggs. Her small pockets were already bulging with eggs, and she handed me two for safekeeping.

I asked if she should leave at least one egg for the poor mother duck.

"It's okay; they always lay new ones," she explained, smiling at my concern.

So far the children had found four nests; Sally and I had found only one. I wondered if that was because the children were closer to the ground. Perhaps it was because we had been distracted by the white globeflowers, pink moss campion, and other flowers that had burst into bloom on the south-facing slopes.

Back at camp, we sampled the different eggs that we had

collected. We were surprised the loon eggs weren't fish-flavoured, even though loons eat only fish. Boiled tern eggs, though, did have fishy-tasting yolks.

"Which eggs do you like best?" I asked Leroy.

"The biggest ones!" Those were the loon eggs; they were almost twice the size of a large chicken egg.

By mid-June, twilight persisted from sunset at eleven until sunrise two hours later. The children went egg hunting at all hours. At any time of day or night, snowmobiles headed across the sea ice, towing qamutiks loaded with adults and children. Young men often stayed out hunting or fishing all night, returning in the early hours of the morning.

When Papaluk's husband went hunting, we often kept her company. Sally helped Papaluk prepare caribou meat to make nipku, the dried meat we had eaten at Mamaaq's. Many times Papaluk set aside her ulu and talked about the old days or shared gossip she'd heard on the CB radio.

A job that would have taken Papaluk only a couple of hours by herself took all afternoon when she was talking to Sally. After reminiscing for a while, Papaluk would resume slicing a lump of meat into long thin strips. Sally would lay out the pieces on the rocks to dry in the warm sun.

Anyone visiting camp was welcome to help themselves to a snack of nipku. People walking through camp would often cut off a chunk of *pipsi*, the rich, oily Arctic char hanging on the tent lines.

One afternoon, I sliced a piece of drying fish from the line and popped it into my mouth. I thought back to my reluctance to try different foods when we had first arrived in Baker Lake. That seemed so long ago. I had learned many new skills throughout the year, but most importantly, I had learned to be more open to new experiences.

"Last fall, you wouldn't have tried that," Sally laughed later, as I polished off a piece of caribou tongue.

As we sat outside basking in the warmth of the evening sun, the cold, dark days of winter seemed so far away. The memories of blizzards and frozen fingers were swept away by the tide of returning warmth and life.

Inuit children at spring camp

Spring camp "on the land"

Although the land had been roused from its long winter sleep, the sea was still covered with a sheet of thick ice. Each day, however, the floe edge crept closer and closer to land. Countless puddles expanded to form a giant lake of emerald green water on the surface of the ice. Heat waves rose from the meltwater and cast magical mirages in the distance. Shimmering islands seemed suspended above the horizon or towered over the ice, stretched by an optical illusion to ten times their actual height.

Eventually the sheet of ice broke into large irregular-shaped pans. At high tide, the floating pans of ice formed a loose pack that shifted with the current. Each time the tide went out, more loose ice was carried away. Blocks of ice two metres high were left stranded on the shore, many tipped at precarious angles. At high tide they had bobbed so gracefully in the water; on land they looked like beached whales, awkward and unable to move.

Papaluk had told us the topmost ice of the towering blocks was salt-free. Reaching for the top of a block, Sally used her ulu to chip ice into her pot. Leroy stood just beside her, his head tilted back, tongue out, to catch drops of water.

The ice stranded on shore became a new playground for the children. Little Annie Kukkiak had claimed a piece of ice as her own high viewpoint, while groups of boys jumped from block to block in their version of an obstacle course. The large blocks also lent themselves well to games of hide-and-seek. We often heard giggles of children just before they jumped out to surprise us as we filled our pots.

At high tide, the Kukkiak children could be found playing on floating ice in the protected bays. Leroy and his cousins claimed pieces of ice at the shore as their boats, gingerly stepping on the ones in the shallow water.

One morning in early July, we woke to hear a child crying outside our tent. I peeked out the door and saw Annie looking out to sea, tears streaming down her face.

"What's wrong, Annie?" I asked.

"My piece of ice is gone!" she said between heaving sobs.

Overnight, the ice had been flushed out by the wind and

outgoing tide. Half a kilometre from shore was a floating band of white ice, and in between was deep-blue water, so soothing to look at after a winter of white. Our reaction was the opposite to Annie's. We were eager to start paddling.

"Maybe you shouldn't go yet," Papaluk said. "The ice will come back when the wind changes."

As Papaluk predicted, the ice did come back. By late that afternoon, an easterly wind had picked up and we heard a dull roar from the beach, like the rolling of thunder. Huge blocks of ice were moving rapidly towards the shore. Waves rolled in and broke on the outer blocks, then continued towards shore, tossing metre-thick pieces of ice onto the beach.

The endless energy of the rolling surf pushed the massive pans of ice back and forth, grinding, buckling, and riding on top of other large pans.

"I'm glad we're not paddling in that!" Sally shouted over the din. The deafening crescendo as the waves crashed over the ice reaffirmed the sea's power and our decision to remain land-bound a while longer.

With so much open water in sight, Sally and I became restless. Before leaving the north, we wanted the experience of travelling on the sea, as the Inuit had done for thousands of years. Paddling along the coast of Hudson Bay would be a formidable challenge in our small canoe, but we felt it would complete our year in the north.

The only way we could safely canoe along the coast was to travel while there were still ice pans floating on Hudson Bay; they would keep the winds from building the sea into huge rollers and swells. However, timing was crucial. We had to wait until most of the ice had broken into smaller pieces—it would be impossible to land the canoe if huge blocks of ice were crashing onto the shore.

Papaluk poked her head into our tent on the morning of July 8, a few days after the ice had made its false departure.

"The ice is gone now," she announced.

When Sally and I went to the shore we noticed that an especially high tide was lifting even the previously land-locked pieces of ice. By afternoon, the outgoing tide and an offshore wind flushed the last ice into Hudson Bay.

Sally and I knew that if we were going to paddle along the coast, we had to leave soon. As we watched the ice drift away, we realized that the time had come for us to drift south as well. We felt sad about leaving our new friends, about leaving the north. It was with mixed feelings that we packed our gear for the canoe trip to Rankin Inlet. Our time in the Arctic was almost over. It had passed all too quickly.

"*Matna, tagvauvutit,* (Thank you, we are going now,)" Sally said to the Kukkiaks the next morning as we pushed the canoe away from the beach. We paddled away slowly, not quite knowing what else to say to our Inuit friends.

Then a slushy snowball splashed into the water beside us.

"You missed, Leroy!" I called, laughing. Our spirits lifted, we dug in with our paddles and began canoeing south.

TWENTY-TWO

Canoeing South

Icebergs towered over our heads, and ghostlike blocks of white appeared then disappeared in the morning fog. As we canoed away from Chesterfield Inlet, the only sounds were the patter of drops from our paddles and the delicate splash of water dripping from the icebergs.

Sally and I had just set out for Rankin Inlet, where we would end our year's journey. It felt good to be back in the canoe, the moulded seat under my backside and a well-balanced paddle in my hands.

Eventually the warm sun dissolved the fog, and every odd-shaped piece of ice cast its mirror image on the water, adding interest to our paddling. The icebergs were shades of green, pale at the top and turning to dark green-blue deep in the water.

By early afternoon, the icebergs began moving out to sea with the ebb tide. Six hours after we began canoeing, we found ourselves paddling into the strong current of the ebb tide.

"No sense fighting the current," I said. We didn't mind the opportunity for a rest; our arms were tired from the first day of paddling. We beached the canoe and spent a lazy afternoon exploring the seashore.

The tide, not the time of day, would determine our paddling routine for the next two weeks. We planned to paddle with the incoming tides, which would carry us south along the coast of Hudson Bay.

The next three days were windy, but floating ice kept the waves to a manageable height. We had expected wind and waves to keep us shore-bound for several days on the way to Rankin Inlet. We hadn't expected to see the pack ice return! The next morning, Sally and I woke to find a strong southeasterly wind had blown ice to shore. We were stranded almost a kilometre from open water. At high tide every piece of ice floated and we considered it too dangerous to launch the canoe.

Finally the wind dropped. The tide had gone out as well, and the ice was no longer such a hazard—much of it lay stranded on the beach. All we had to do was get the canoe across a shoulder-high obstacle course of jumbled ice to the open water.

"We should be able to drag the canoe across this," I said, studying the mass of ice.

"Loaded?" Sally asked sceptically, eyeing the bruised and battered hull of our canoe.

"Sure, why not? Think of the rocks we dragged it over last summer!"

After lifting the empty canoe onto the shelf of ice, we loaded all our gear. Then Sally pushed on the stern of the heavily loaded canoe while I pulled on a long rope attached to the bow. She winced each time the canoe crashed into hollows on the uneven ice. I gritted my teeth when I heard a loud *crack!* from the hull as the canoe teetered on a high spot.

Once we reached the floating ice, moving the loaded canoe became even more difficult. Gingerly, I stepped onto a block of ice. It held my weight. Feeling a little more confident, I stepped onto the next block. It sank, nearly filling my boot with frigid water. I quickly jumped back to safety.

"Some people never learn," Sally said, laughing. "I seem to remember your last swim was a bit chilly."

We tested each piece of ice by pushing down on it with our paddles before jumping from pan to pan. There was no way of telling which ice blocks were thick and which were eroded underneath and ready to flip bottom-up. Leaning on the gunnels of the canoe, we picked our way across the ice, stopping every step to pull the canoe ahead.

At the edge of the open water, the swells made launching the canoe a challenge. As we studied the rhythm of the swells, we decided to jump into the canoe as soon as a swell passed. We hoped to be under power before the next one had a chance to drive us against the ice. It worked!

"Pull, pull!" I encouraged Sally. In unison, we powered the canoe into the waves. The finely tuned teamwork that we had developed last summer was second nature to us.

Later that day we encountered ice that stretched as far as we could see. We thought we'd have to wait for several days for the wind to change direction and move the ice out. As it turned out, the ice wasn't solid and we worked our way along narrow passages between the pans of ice. It was like canoeing across a giant, floating jigsaw puzzle.

We weren't alone among the pans of ice. "Follow those whiskers!" directed Sally, pointing her paddle towards a gleaming, whiskered face that peered at us from between the ice pans. Just as I dipped my paddle into the water, the seal dived.

"Lost it," I said.

"No, we didn't—it's over there." The seal had reappeared in another patch of open water. It was playing with us, always luring us onward but never letting us get close enough for a photograph.

Sally and I also shared the icy passage with flocks of sea birds. Eider ducks roosted on the floating ice, gulls wheeled and turned in the air, and black guillemots bobbed in the water.

A roar of flapping wings echoed across the water as a flock of eider ducks suddenly took flight. Holding our breaths and

Wrestling our canoe across the ice

Canoeing among icebergs

staring in awe, we watched the large iceberg they had been resting on turn bottom-up. A wave of water caused by the tipping iceberg rushed towards us. We were lucky that the wave wasn't big enough to swamp the canoe.

After that, we picked a route that took us past low pans of ice and avoided the towering bergs that had been eroded by waves. Many icebergs resembled distorted hourglasses; it was only a matter of time before they too would roll over. The slowly dissolving hourglass shape of the icebergs reminded us that our time in the Arctic was almost at an end. I noticed that we had unconsciously slowed our paddling tempo. We were in no hurry to get to our destination, for once we reached Rankin Inlet our trip would be over.

Sally and I waited for the early afternoon low tide before starting to paddle on our last day. After lugging our gear a kilometre to the water, we loaded the canoe while the incoming tide lapped at our ankles. It was a race to load everything before the creeping water reached our pile of bags on the beach.

As we canoed over shallow, rocky reefs, the incoming tide surged over the rocks. Many times we were startled by a sudden roar from behind us, and turned to see a huge wave bearing down on the canoe. I glanced at the map; this area of turbulent water was the same place where, four months earlier, we had dealt with towering pressure ridges of ice.

By nine o'clock that evening we were only ten kilometres from the settlement of Rankin Inlet.

"It's a beautiful evening. Let's keep paddling," Sally suggested. The water was unruffled by wind or waves, so I readily agreed.

The sun dipped below the horizon just before eleven o'clock, painting the sky a rich red. For the next two hours the sky slowly faded to soft peach, then brightened to yellow as the rising sun moved towards the horizon, not far from where it had set.

It was after one o'clock in the morning when we left the shelter of an island and headed across the last stretch of open water. As always, we worried about getting caught in a wind when paddling across an unprotected stretch of water, even if only a kilometre wide.

The winds of the Arctic had the last word. There wasn't far to go when a strong gale came up without warning. Within minutes it whipped the calm water into large waves. We paddled and paddled but appeared to be getting nowhere. Sally and I discussed returning to the barren island, but I worried that we'd be stranded there for many days with no fresh water.

We were running diagonally into the waves and each time one hit us, I was thankful for the foot-controlled rudder. Without the rudder we would have been mercilessly tossed about and pushed in every direction—except where we wanted to go. I had to fight the pressure on the rudder to keep us on course.

"Keep going, kiddo, we're just about there!" Sally encouraged me.

Struggling against white-capped waves that splashed over the bow of the canoe and drenched Sally, we paddled towards shore. For almost an hour, the wind and waves conspired to push us backwards.

As we pulled together towards the shore, I realized that we were at our best in situations like this. We both knew that each of us was giving it everything we had. Perhaps it was this sense of trust, of teamwork, that we would remember most about our year in the north. Through the difficult times and challenges of the trip, we had grown even closer together.

Finally we made it to our destination. All through the year, the wind had been our constant adversary. Battling the wind one last time seemed a fitting end to our Arctic journey.

We pulled our canoe out of the water for the last time. Wordlessly, I gave Sally a big hug.

"Adventure we wanted, adventure we found...right to the last day!" she said, her eyes shining with excitement.

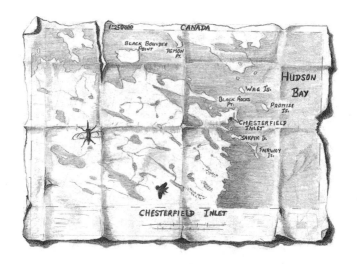

Epilogue

I unfolded the map that had accompanied us along the coast of Hudson Bay, first by dog team, then by canoe. It was no longer the clean sheet we had studied in the outfitter's shop more than a year earlier. Now it told a story . . . peanut butter from a snack in one place, blood from the dog fight on another.

Memories flooded back as we looked at other maps. On the map of Baker Lake, we saw where Mamaaq had taken us fishing, and we remembered the special times we had spent with her. "Blizzard" scrawled on a map of the coast summoned images of the three long days we had spent in an igloo. Other words triggered memories of travelling through deep snow with our team of Huskies.

Sally opened another map and dried-out corpses of black flies tumbled out.

"Remember the bugs?" Sally asked, grimacing. "How about a few in your tea for old times' sake?"

The map from our first summer was peppered with bugs, and a flattened mosquito was preserved in every detail. Other maps had water marks and tattered corners. "Ledges and Rocks" seemed like too few words to describe the excitement of careening down the wild Thelon River.

After thirteen months and thirty-five hundred kilometres, we had completed our Arctic adventures. It had been a journey through seasons, through time, and across a vast land. It had also been a journey to another culture, a journey of learning.

I looked over at Sally. Like the maps, we had changed. Sally's face was tanned, her hair tousled by the wind. My knee still had a scar where I had been bitten in the dog fight. Both of us had hands that were callused from paddling, and Sally's fingertips were still sensitive to cold.

Sally and I had changed in other ways as well. The process of turning our dream into reality had tested and forged our relationship. As we met each challenge, we had surprised ourselves and each other with new-found strengths. Sally had overcome her fear of dogs. I had learned from Mamaaq to open my heart and mind to a different way of life. We came north looking for adventure; we had found that and much more.

I knew the memories of our trip would live on through slide shows and our writing. Those were for later; for now, it was the maps that told the story. I retraced our route with my finger, more confidently than I had when the maps were new and untattered. We had done it after all.

"The old-timer was right," I said to Sally. "It does look easy on the map."

"Well, even if the map had warned us about what really lay ahead, we would have done it anyway!" Sally said, laughing.

I refolded the maps . . . for now, we were leaving the north behind. There would be new maps to follow another year. They too would have a story to tell at the end of the journey, perhaps of a long horseback trip to the Yukon or a canoe trip down another Arctic river. Sally and I both knew the north would lure us back again.

FROM THE AUTHORS

Thank you for joining us on our journey to the Arctic. If you shivered during the winter blizzards or cringed when our qamutik broke through the ice, then we know you were with us, in spirit if not in body. We hope you enjoyed reading about our adventures as much as we enjoyed recounting them.

Sally and I would like to invite you to share our other adventures. Our first book, *Wilderness Seasons*, is our story of living in the wilderness of northern British Columbia for fourteen months. Together, we built a small log cabin and shared the trials and triumphs of a life far from civilization. We wrote this book a few years ago, and if a bookstore doesn't have it in stock the store can order it for you. We're sure you'll enjoy escaping from the city for a while and joining us in the wilderness.

For our second book, *Wild and Free*, we spent several years photographing wildlife in the north. While Sally got as close as possible to sketch each animal, I peered through the viewfinder of a camera to get face-to-snout photographs. Along the way, we were chased by angry bull elk, were befriended by porcupines, and had several close encounters with bears. We think you'll enjoy our adventures and misadventures. If your local bookstore doesn't have this book on the shelf, we're sure your bookseller would be pleased to order it for you.

What's next? We're planning a year-long trip by canoe and horseback through the remote wilderness of northern British Columbia and the Yukon. We don't know anything about horses, saddles, or pack-boxes . . . but that's part of the challenge!

Ian and Sally Wilson,
July 1992

ACKNOWLEDGEMENTS

The following organizations and companies assisted us with our journey. To all, we are most grateful for their financial assistance, product contributions, and, most of all, their faith in our expedition:

Our principal thanks goes to British Columbia Television for their financial contribution and their enthusiastic support of our adventure.

Molson Breweries for their sponsorship of our adventure.

Altamira Investment Services for their sponsorship of our trip.

Canadian Northern Shield Insurance for their sponsorship.

Travel Keewatin for their support and encouragement.

Ralston Purina for their contribution of High Energy Dog Chow that kept our seven hungry Huskies fueled for the trip.

Marlin and Mary Bayes of Western Canoeing for crafting our canoe and rudder assembly.

Coleman Canada for supplying us with our Peak 1 camp stoves; these stoves never failed us, even in the coldest weather.

Brian Dorfman of Grey Owl Paddles, who provided us with lightweight, hand-crafted paddles.

Tilley Endurables for supplying us with indestructible pants and shirts, and hats that floated!

Andrea Dillon & Associates for the Karhu skis we used for our adventures to the floe edge, as well as the excellent Merrell hiking boots.

Stanfield's for donating Polartherm underwear and wool long johns that kept us cozy through the long, cold winter.

Sherpa Industries for the Berwin Bindings we used on our cross-country skis.

Jim Nason of Lucerne Foods for his enthusiastic support and for supplies ranging from peanut butter to macaroni dinners.

Ken Jones of Jones Leisure Wear for his continued support and for supplying down parkas and sleeping bags.

NWT Air for flying our boxes of food and equipment across the Northwest Territories.

Far West Industries for their excellent Gore-Tex parkas.

Rogers Foods for their nine-grain cereal, granola, and flour.

Cascade Designs for supplying us with Therm-a-rest sleeping mats and waterproof Cascade bags.

Spilsbury Communications for lending us an SBX11 radio for emergency communication.

North Face for the VE25 expedition tent.

Many people helped us along the way. Without their support our expedition would have been much more difficult, and sometimes downright impossible. We would like to thank the following people:

Mamaaq Innakatsik and her family in Baker Lake for adopting us, and for teaching us so much about Inuit life.

Henry Ford for all his help and open-armed welcome to Baker Lake.

Joanne Dionne of Chesterfield Inlet for her warm friendship and a place to stay.

Bernard Krako in Chesterfield Inlet for teaching us about dogsledding.

Wally Du Temple for putting up with dogs and qamutik-building in his house at Chesterfield Inlet!

Barry Amarok in Chesterfield Inlet for sharing his house with us.

Alan Everard for his generous hospitality in Rankin Inlet.

Remi Nokkitok and his family in Rankin Inlet for all their help.

Leah Innakatsik for a warm place to stay in Whale Cove.

Lynne Rollin and her dog, Kuni, for their friendship in Arviat.

Jeffrey Dinsdale for his enthusiasm and tips about dogsledding.

Bill Carpenter for his advice about dogs and dogsledding.

Gord Stewart at Braden-Burry Expediting for somehow getting everything to us!

Bob and Anne Wilson for being our expedition support crew!

G L O S S A R Y

Inuktitut words are given in the Baker Lake dialect and may be different in other settlements.

ajagaak	A game consisting of a small hollow bone attached by a string to a peg.
amauti	Woman's parka featuring a back pouch to carry a baby, and a hood to pull over the heads of the mother and child.
atigi	Caribou-skin inner parka with fur facing inwards.
atii	Let's go; go ahead (two of several meanings).
ayarak	A string game similar to cat's cradle.
hakuut	A tool for scraping caribou hides.
howa-ii	The command we used to turn our dog team right.
hulla	The command we used to turn our dog team left.
igloo	A snow shelter.
Igluliarjuk	Chesterfield Inlet.
igluliniartunga	I will teach you to build an igloo.
ii	Yes.
ikii	It is cold!
iliniartuq	To learn by doing.
imaq	Water.
Inuit	"The People"; the native people living in the Arctic. Plural of Inuk.
Inuk	"One of the People"; a native person living in the Arctic.
inukshuk	A stone structure, often built to resemble the form of a person.
Inuktitut	Language of the Inuit.
iqtuqhit	A tool for stretching caribou hides.
iqualuit	Many fish, or place of many fish.
ivalu	Caribou sinew (used for thread).
kajak	A canoe or kayak.
kamik	A boot made from sealskin or caribou skin.
kinauvit	What is your name?

matna	Thank you.
miqsuq	To sew.
naaq	Stomach.
namuqtuq	It doesn't matter.
nani nunaqaqpit	What place did you come from?
naugli	Where is . . . ?
nauk	No.
nietna	Like this.
nipku	Dried caribou meat.
nugluktuq	A game in which the players try to poke small spears through a hole drilled into a suspended piece of antler or bone.
oubloumi	Today.
pipsi	Dried fish.
piqsiqtuq	It is a blizzard.
qablu	Eyebrow(s).
Qablunaaq	Person from the south.
qaigit	Come here.
qamutik	A long sled.
qimuksiq	Dogsledding.
qimuksiq oubloumi	Would you like to go dogsledding today?
qulittaq	Caribou-skin outer parka with the fur facing outwards.
qulliq	A soapstone lamp in which oil is burned for light and heat.
quviasukvik	A time to be happy; Christmas.
quyanami	It can't be helped.
tagvauvutit	We are going now.
taima	I am finished; or it is finished.
taku	Look (one of several meanings).
tapsi	A sash tied around a caribou parka.
teagukpin	Would you like tea?
tiguaq	Adopted child.
tiqirq	Thimble or index finger.
ukiaq	Autumn.
ulu	Curved woman's knife.
unakuluk	You're a naughty one!

INDEX

Also by Ian and Sally Wilson

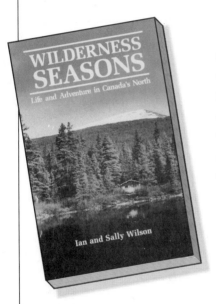

Wilderness Seasons is an inspiring account of Ian and Sally Wilson's year in remote wilderness, more than 200 kilometres from the nearest settlement or road. From the challenge of building a hand-hewn log cabin to the intimacy of moose breath at three metres, Ian and Sally share the trials and triumphs of a life close to nature.

A NATIONAL BESTSELLER
208 pages ISBN 0-919574-34-3
$14.95

Wild and Free is a mix of stunning photography, detailed drawings, and personal encounters with wildlife in Canada's north. Mountain climbing with goats, petting porcupines, and meeting burly black bears are just some of the adventures the authors share. Each chapter is a blend of interesting facts and personal observations, told in a warm, entertaining way.

A NATIONAL BESTSELLER
192 pages ISBN 0-919574-87-4
$14.95

Both published by Gordon Soules Book Publishers Ltd.